Third Man in the Ring

Related Titles from Potomac Books

My Life and Battles
—Jack Johnson, translated and edited by Christopher Rivers

Boxing's Most Wanted™: The Top 10 Book of Champs, Chumps, and Punch-Drunk Palookas
—Mike Fitzgerald and David L. Hudson Jr.

Rocky Lives! Heavyweight Boxing Upsets of the 1990s
—David E. Finger

Mixed Martial Arts' Most Wanted™: The Top 10 Book of Crazy Combat, Great Grappling, and Sick Submissions
—Adam T. Heath and David L. Hudson Jr.

Third
Man in the Ring

33 of Boxing's Best Referees and Their Stories

MIKE FITZGERALD and **PATRICK MORLEY**

Potomac Books
Washington, D.C.

Library of Congress Cataloging-in-Publication Data
Fitzgerald, Mike, 1965–
    Third man in the ring : 33 of boxing's best referees and their stories / Mike Fitzgerald and Patrick Morley.
        pages cm.
    ISBN 978-1-61234-224-5 (hardcover : alk. paper)
    ISBN 978-1-61234-242-9 (electronic)
    1. Boxing. 2. Boxing—Anecdotes. 3. Boxing referees—Anecdotes. I. Title.
    GV1135.F54 2013
    796.82—dc23

                                                                    2012043854

Printed in the United States of America on acid-free paper that meets the American National Standards Institute Z39-48 Standard.

Potomac Books
22841 Quicksilver Drive
Dulles, Virginia 20166

First Edition

10 9 8 7 6 5 4 3 2 1

CONTENTS

FOREWORD

David Hudson Jr.

As a boxing judge, I have the utmost respect for referees, who have the most difficult and dangerous job among all officials in the sweet science. Boxing judges must concentrate, block out crowd noise, and focus on the quantity and quality of clean, effective punching. We are only noticed if we issue controversial scorecards. As daunting as that may be, a referee faces a much more formidable task.

The referee must protect the fighters' safety, administer the rules, break apart the fighters, and maintain order in the ring. A referee doesn't have the luxury of sitting in a high-standing chair right at ringside like a boxing judge. The referee occupies center stage in the ring and must exert considerable energy in navigating around it. Their duties are awe-inspiring. Fighters' lives can depend on referees' ultimate decision on whether to stop a fight or allow it to continue. The pressure is palpable and the exchanges with cornermen are intense. It takes a special person to be the third man in the ring.

I've had the privilege of working with some fine referees in world title bouts, including a match in South Africa by Howard John Foster, who is featured in a chapter of this book. I watched as Foster flawlessly refereed the action, and I later discussed with him the lengthy commitment that it took for him to reach a star-grade referee in his homeland.

Authors Mike Fitzgerald and Patrick Morley provide boxing fans with a veritable treasure trove of stories about thirty-three boxing referees—men who have refereed some of the most significant bouts in boxing history. No boxing book has provided the sport's aficionados with anything this comprehensive—examining the careers and career highlights of these top international third men in the ring.

As a longtime follower of boxing, I enjoyed reading about all the referees, and it brought back some memories reading about the historical bouts discussed by Mills Lane, Richard Steele, Carlos Padilla, and Frank Cappuccino, as well more recent mega-fights worked by some of the game's current top referees and their bouts featuring Mike Tyson, Oscar De La Hoya, Manny Pacquiao, and Floyd Mayweather.

There also is an interesting chapter on MMA's legendary referee "Big" John McCarthy who describes his entry into professional boxing and discusses his viewpoints on officiating in boxing and MMA and his observation on the two sports. Many sports fans feel like boxing is "on the ropes" as far as popularity. Boxing has been around for a while, and it is not going anywhere. It is here to stay.

These referees are all true professionals in the ring, and their dedication to the craft shines through in this book. Readers will not only learn about the major world title bouts they've worked but also how these officials first entered into the addictive sport of boxing. Some officiated in other sports, others started in the amateur ranks after their fighting careers ended, and others gravitated to the sport later in life. Their stories differ greatly as some of the more colorful characters featured in this book delve into their shenanigans outside of the ring as well. I laughed out loud while reading about the antics of characters like Mickey Vann and Bruce McTavish and their adventures while on international assignments.

Coauthor Mike Fitzgerald worked with me in the writing of the boxing book titled *Boxing's Most Wanted™: The Top Ten Book of Champs, Chumps, and Punch-Drunk Palookas*. And I enjoyed the effort put forward in this gem that Mike coauthored with Patrick Morley.

I recently had the privilege of meeting Pat at a boxing official's convention in Las Vegas. He is a walking, talking encyclopedia of boxing. He shares

Mike's infectious enthusiasm for the sweet science. You can feel and almost hear their love of the sport reverberating through the pages of this great read. As world-class boxing judges, Mike and Pat know about boxing. They know and appreciate the sacrifices of the third man in the ring.

Read this book, enjoy it, and cherish it. You will find yourself hoping that Mike and Pat write a sequel with even more referees' stories. I know I do.

FOREWORD

Harold Lederman

Okay fight fans! As long as I can recall, I have always loved boxing. I started judging in 1967, and before that I attended as many boxing matches as possible. Through my years as a ringside judge and now as HBO's "Unofficial Official" I have been asked why I never became a referee. I guess I was happy and felt more comfortable being a judge, but I have worked with some of boxing history's most accomplished referees, many of whom are featured in this book and are good friends of mine. *Third Man in the Ring* brought back so many memories of the great experiences that I have had with a number of the referees featured in this book.

I had the privilege of being a judge several times in Las Vegas when Carlos Padilla was the third man in the ring. Two bouts that stand out to me occurred in 1985, when Larry Holmes defended his title against David Bey, and later that year when he suffered his first defeat at the hands of Michael Spinks. Padilla did an excellent job in both of those fights.

Years earlier, Padilla refereed the "Thrilla in Manila" in the Philippines, between Muhammad Ali and Joseph "Smokin' Joe" Frazier. It was interesting to learn about Padilla's selection as referee for that legendary bout, as then president Ferdinand Marcos had requested a local referee. Here was someone so dedicated to his craft that he later relocated to Las Vegas just to referee in the "capital" of boxing.

The chapter about my old friend Mills Lane brought back some wonderful memories. He was one of the best in the sport and my association with him goes back to August 1981, when we worked a world title fight together in Seoul, South Korea. In 1986, I began working for HBO and unofficially judged many of the championship matches that Lane would referee.

Currently my job is to be as objective as possible when scoring fights on HBO, but I don't have to be objective about stating that the thirty-three referees represented in this book are some of boxing history's finest.

Fight fans will also be able to read about some of my other colleagues, like Frank Cappuccino, whom I worked with many times in Atlantic City, New Jersey. He discusses the Mike Tyson vs. Michael Spinks bout he refereed as well as how he threatened to break a mobster's jaw in his early days refereeing in Philadelphia.

While the sport of boxing will always remain significant, the popularity of Mixed Martial Arts (MMA) has increased. Two of the referees featured in this book, "Big" John McCarthy and Tony Weeks, have also obtained champion status as officials in MMA. McCarthy is one of the sport's most accomplished referees, and Weeks works as a judge. Despite MMA's rise to prominence boxing will always be around. And who knows? With a few hot heavyweight prospects the sport could always return to the popularity it once had.

There are other referees featured in this book that don't have a high profile name, possibly only due to their current zip code, but are top fight world class referees whose stories made for an enjoyable read. I once judged a world title fight in Acapulco, Mexico, that was refereed by Minnesota's Denny Nelson. He and his son Mark both share their international adventures in this book. I remember seeing Mark at officials' seminars when he was just a kid tagging along with his dad. He's developed into one of the world's best referees.

I have enjoyed reading about some other colleagues of mine featured in *Third Man in the Ring* and I think you will too as they share their diverse backgrounds, what it took for them to reach the pinnacle of their profession, and the unique experiences arbitrating world championship boxing matches either televised live or abroad.

FOREWORD

Tim Lueckenhoff

Executive Director, Missouri Office of Athletics;
President, Association of Boxing Commissions (ABC)

A boxing referee is the single most important official involved in boxing. He or she is the person who will protect not only the fighter's health, safety, and welfare, but a referee also protects the financial interest of the promoters, managers, and the fighters. Referees ensure all bouts are fair. Referees have to learn how to quickly assess a boxer to know when he or she has received too much punishment and it is time to stop a fight. This can be a very difficult process to master and only comes with experience in the ring and watching other referees work bouts. With the crowd noise and other interested parties yelling and screaming for their contestant, a referee's level of concentration must be at its best. Whenever I am questioned about a referee's decision, I am always quick to explain that a referee is the person who is concentrating 100 percent of the time during a fight. Sometimes they are so close to the bout that it is difficult to see low blows, butts, holding, and other fouling on the opposite side of the fighters, but as long as a referee is fair in his assessment of action in the ring, those actions usually do not interfere with the flow of a bout. All referees must continue to work four-round preliminary fights and stay active on a regular basis to hone their skills. The best referees are those that have a humble personality, appreciate their assignments regardless of the magnitude, and are truly impartial officials who enforce the rules equally for each boxer.

ACKNOWLEDGMENTS

The authors would like to first acknowledge the thirty-three world-class referees for lending their time, insight, wisdom, and experience to this project. Thank you for all you do to make boxing the wonderful sport it is, and for keeping boxers safe as possible.

Many thanks are due, in alphabetical order, to the following people for their contributions to this project: Pete Ehrmann, Steve Farhood, Charlie Fitch, Ted Gimza, David Hudson, Jerry Jakubco, Tommy Lane, Harold Lederman, Ted Lerner, Tim Lueckenhoff, Bob Lynch, Joe Pasquale, Alexis Ramos, Jeanette Salazar, and Lindsey Tucker.

We would also like to thank our families, with a special thanks to our wives, Deb Fitzgerald and Chantall Morley, for their support of the book.

1

Phil Austin

On September 3, 2011, the Republic of Armenia in Eurasia hosted its first professional boxing card. The main event in the capital city of Yerevan featured native son Vic Darchinyan, a three-division champion and 2000 Olympian, defending his International Boxing Organization (IBO) bantamweight title against Evans Mbamba of South Africa.

Like other former Russian satellite countries, tiny Armenia had experienced growing pains and economic problems since the Soviet Union dissolved twenty years earlier. But eight thousand proud Armenians, including President Serzh Sargsyan, turned out to cheer for their national idol in the fight at the Karen Demirchyan Sports and Concerts Complex.

The referee on this historic occasion was Phil Austin, a well-known boxing official who'd refereed title fights in his adopted home of Australia, as well as abroad, for more than fifteen years. He'd worked high-profile bouts featuring former world champions, including Anthony Mundine, Philip Holiday, and John "The Beast" Mugabi, and served as a judge for fights involving ring legends Ricky Hatton and Joe Bugner.

But none of that prepared him for what he encountered in Armenia.

The government there spared little expense, flying in Austin and other members of the Australian National Boxing Federation to oversee the arrangements for the fight. There was no boxing commission in Armenia. There wasn't even a boxing ring—the Australians brought that, too.

When Austin arrived at the airport in Yerevan a crowd of enthusiastic Darchinyan fans was on hand to welcome him. People wanted their photos taken with him, and one even produced a bottle of vodka and proposed that Austin join them in the celebration that had obviously started long before he arrived on the scene.

"I felt bad about declining their offer," said Austin, "but I don't drink. Besides, I was there to do a job and not be a part of the show."

After Darchinyan made his boisterous fans even happier by winning a unanimous twelve-round decision over Mbamba, he dedicated his victory to the twentieth anniversary of Armenia's independence and presented his title belt to President Sargsyan.

"Vic is like a rock star there, and the fight was like a national holiday," said Austin. "The atmosphere was terrific, and the crowd showed a great love for the fighters who had just given them twelve hard rounds of action. After the fight, everyone wanted my photo because I had just refereed their national hero. It was a great experience, and they can never take this one away from me!"

Austin owes it all to the sport of cricket. Though born in Singapore, he grew up in London's East End. His mother's side of the family boasted lots of boxers, but she didn't like the sport and discouraged Phil's participation in it. When Austin was ten, his dad retired from the Second Air Force and the family moved to New Zealand. Austin started playing cricket and did some amateur boxing, but his boxing days ended when he was struck in the eye with a cricket ball. "The injury was serious enough that I said, 'Enough of this,' and then directed my sporting interests toward becoming a judge and referee in amateur boxing," he said. "That cricket ball actually did me a hell of a favor."

Austin joined the Canterbury Boxing Association and met Zane McDonald, a top Kiwi referee who became his mentor. In 1992, Austin got his license as an amateur referee and judge. The ten-year-old boys he refereed in his third-man-in-the-ring debut probably weren't as nervous as he was. "My knees were shaking, but everything worked out fine," he said.

In 1995, Austin moved to Brisbane, Australia, where he still lives with his wife, Sonia, and his two sons, Connor and Cameron. There he continued to work in the amateurs and found a new mentor in Derek Milham, a referee and secretary of the Queensland boxing commission. "I did some judging on cards for a few months, and Derek helped me progress and was very giving of his time," said Austin. "After every fight I judged or refereed, I went to Derek for his opinion."

On November 11 of that year, Austin worked his first pro bout, a scheduled four-round contest between Brad Drennan and Benny Hopkins. It lasted less than a round, with Austin stopping it after Hopkins went down twice. The biggest cheers—thanks to Phil's then-fiancée Sonia—were for the referee. "I had to tell her afterwards that the tradition is to boo the ref, not cheer him!" he said with a laugh.

In the late 1990s, former World Boxing Council (WBC) junior middleweight champion John "The Beast" Mugabi moved to Australia to resurrect his career. After a few comeback wins in Queensland, he was matched with Paul Smallman on February 26, 1998. Austin got the call to referee. "I thought to myself, *That guy is something special, and to be refereeing one of his fights, it can't get much better than this,*" stated Austin, although he thought differently by the end of the fight, which Mugabi won by decision.

When "The Beast" kept winging punches near the close of the early rounds, Austin ended up literally leaping between the fighters to make sure that no damage was done after the bell. None was—except to him. "Mugabi landed one right on my elbow," Austin recalled. "He sure hadn't lost his punch, and my whole arm went numb. It didn't make collecting the scorecards between rounds any easier!"

In 2001, Australian John Wayne Parr was the first Westerner to win Thailand's esteemed King's Cup as a Muay Thai fighter. The colorful Parr, who was also 8-1 as a traditional boxer, was called The Gunslinger, and when introduced would pantomime fast-drawing a gun in the fashion of his famous namesake. Austin was the referee when Parr fought former Pakistani Olympian Rasheed Baloch for the Oceanic Boxing Association's light middleweight title.

"Parr was dropped early in the fight, but by the time I got to 'six' he had regained his senses and told me he was fine," recollected Austin. "He went on to take Rasheed's heart, and won the fight in the fifth round. Parr was one of the true characters of the sport. I always enjoyed refereeing guys like him."

Acclaimed Aussie rugby player–turned–boxer Tony "The Man" Mundine's Queensland fight with Juarne Dowling on October 14, 2004, was refereed by Austin. All of Mundine's pro fights had been broadcast to massive Australian pay-per-view TV audiences, and before Austin entered the ring he thought about all the hard work it had taken him to get there. "That was where I'd always hoped to be someday as a referee," indicated Austin. "It was worth putting up with all the politics and headaches along the way."

In the third round, Dowling went down hard, and as Austin was counting, Mundine's handlers started to enter the ring, figuring the fight was over. But the downed fighter started to rise, and they had to hustle back out. Austin averted a huge controversy by keeping his head and not disqualifying Mundine for his handlers' premature action. He ended up calling the fight in favor of Mundine in that round anyway.

"During a bout the boxing ring is mine," said Austin. "I control it. I try to always focus on what I'm doing and make as few as mistakes as possible. I'm given a great responsibility in the ring. I have two people's health and careers in my hands. I owe it to them to give them my best. The welfare of the boxers is primary; everything else is secondary. If a fight's only going one way, I'll tell the losing fighter that he needs to show me something. At the end of the day, I want both boxers to get out safely.

"If a cornerman starts yelling at me during a round, I walk over to him after the bell and let him know that if he screams at me I will ignore him. If he has a concern he can bring it to my attention between rounds. I have seen referees fall into a trap by arguing with and being manipulated by cornermen when they should be on top of the action."

Austin's first world title fight was on November 4, 2006, in the Johannesburg suburb of Kempton Park, South Africa. The IBO's minimum weight belt was at stake, and Nkosinathi Joyi won it by knocking out Armando dela Cruz in the second round.

He returned to South Africa a year later to referee Joyi's title defense against Gabriel Pumar in Port Elizabeth. This one ended in the first round when the champion caught Pumar with a shot to the ribs. Austin said he still gets chills remembering how the capacity crowd sang the champion's name in and out of the ring that night.

Austin got a different kind of chill when he went back in South Africa for Joyi's defense against Mexico's Lorenzo Trejo on November 22, 2008. Because of the promoter's financial difficulties, the fight was up in the air. Joyi and Trejo weighed in, but then it was announced that the fight was off. After outraged ticket-holders stormed the Mdantsane Indoor Sport Centre, the fight was hastily rescheduled for the next day, and Joyi anticlimatically stopped his challenger in the second round.

For his fourth assignment in South Africa, Austin refereed the IBO super middleweight title fight between Isaac Chilemba and Thomas Oosthuizen on November 6, 2010. Things heated up when the fighters almost came to blows at a pre-fight charity function, and in their respective dressing rooms before the match, Austin admonished them to leave their animosity there and conduct themselves like professionals in the ring. They fought cleanly and skillfully to a draw, and afterward the promoter congratulated him on "a brilliant job."

Austin has only disqualified two boxers in his professional career. "One of them kept holding, and when I warned him to stop he threw a jab that landed on my chin," Austin said. "He was obviously looking for an easy way out, and I didn't hesitate to give it to him."

Like the mentors who helped him along the way, he takes every opportunity to assist young refs who are just breaking into the game. "If I help someone and they eventually go further than me in the sport, I have contributed to boxing in a positive way," he said. "If capable referees don't get an opportunity to advance, the sport of boxing suffers because of it."

Because the IBO gave him his first international shot, Austin has been loyal to the organization. In addition to refereeing, the real estate agent frequently serves as an IBO supervisor at title fights in Australia and Asia.

California-based referee Jack Reiss calls Austin "one of the best boxing supervisors in the world, a straight-shooter who pulls no punches with promoters, managers, cornermen, and fighters. You always know where you stand with Phil. He expects only the best from his officials, because he cares about the fighters and because he gives his best at all times."

2

Rudy Battle

Pennsylvania State Athletic Commissioner Rudy Battle, the classy former top-tier referee, has had a lifetime of accomplishments. He has been with the commission since 2008, overseeing boxing and mixed martial arts (MMA) in the state that includes Philadelphia—the hard, gritty city that invokes images of tough sports fans, "Smokin'" Joe Frazier, Bernard Hopkins, and fictional boxing hero Rocky Balboa.

But it was in another sport where Battle first made his mark—fencing. A former internationally ranked fencer and National College Athletic Association (NCAA) director of fencing, he initially took on boxing as a new challenge and a way to stay in shape.

In high school, Battle was a state fencing champion. After high school, he served his country as a member of the U.S. Air Force. He was involved in intelligence, with top security clearance, but also got into boxing, since he had been an amateur fighter. He coached the U.S. Air Force team stationed in Northern Japan and led them to the top of the Far East military championships.

As a boxing coach, Battle led by example. "I was always the first one up. I did roadwork along with my team. We had a team concept. That is how we ended up with the most championships. I was able to tell who was working hard on their roadwork, who was not keeping up. Other coaches would tell their fighters to go do roadwork, and then wake them up when they were done to train."

Battle, who is modest about his athletic achievements, commented, "Not many people knew of my boxing and coaching background. And often I hear cornermen and trainers giving their fighters the wrong advice, doing the wrong things, not letting their fighter breathe right. But they would resent me if I told them how to do things right, how to do their job. But that does not prevent them from telling me how to do my job," he added, noting that people always are telling the referee what to do and always have opinions on his performance.

After completing his service in the air force, Battle returned to his first love, fencing. For the next decade, he trained at the University of Pennsylvania under the Olympic team's fencing coach. He won a gold medal, two silver medals, and a bronze medal in national team competitions.

"For ten years, that was my life, fencing. The season starts in September. Four or five days a week, you train, and you compete on weekends. In July, you have the nationals. So you only really had the end of July and August off, before the season started in September." When Battle finally left active competition he became NCAA's director of fencing, a post he served for more than three years, traveling and overseeing fencing competitions.

After leaving the sport, Battle wanted to become involved in another athletic endeavor. "I just didn't want to come home and do nothing," he said, so he turned in a résumé to the Pennsylvania boxing commission to become a referee. The commission was impressed with his athletic accomplishments and his boxing background but wanted him to work the amateurs first. In less than a year, he moved to the professional ranks and made his debut at The legendary Blue Horizon in Philadelphia, a venue once named by *The Ring* magazine as the "best place to watch a boxing match."

When he started out, Battle told his wife his goal was to work "TV shows like the referees did out in Las Vegas." That goal quickly became a reality, "when Vegas came out east," to Atlantic City, New Jersey. The 1980s were the glory days of Atlantic City boxing. At that time, Atlantic City was a boomtown, with new casinos popping up, and plenty of televised boxing. There were hundreds of shows in his neighboring state of New Jersey, with an average of 130 shows a year from 1982 to 1985. The Tropicana Hotel hosted weekly fight cards. Often, televised network TV fights were held on both Saturday and Sunday.

Battle submitted an application to the New Jersey Athletic Commission, whose chairman at the time was the great "Jersey Joe" Walcott, the hall-of-fame former heavyweight champion. Walcott accepted Battle's application and allowed him to get started. His first assignment was a televised fight. Battle soon became a staple of Atlantic City boxing, which allowed him to officiate many title fights, all over the world, for many sanctioning bodies. He is proud that he never had to ask or apply to be a member of these bodies—they always recruited him.

Battle refereed title fights throughout North America, as well as in South America, Europe, Africa, Asia, and Australia. He refereed the first title fight in an Eastern bloc country, the International Boxing Federation (IBF) welterweight title bout between champion Simon Brown and challenger Jorge Maysonet, held in Budapest, Hungary, on February 18, 1989. Brown retained his title by a third round technical knockout. "They shipped out a bunch of mini American flags for people to wave in the audience. Those flags were intercepted at the border, and never made their way to the arena," Battle remembered.

Battle also refereed the first world title fight in Russia. Russia had always been an Olympic powerhouse in boxing, but the USSR had not allowed its fighters to turn professional, as professional sports of any type were prohibited. On July 16, 1993, Battle was the third man in the ring in a historic fight between champion Al "Ice" Cole of the United States and former titlist Glenn McCrory of England for the IBF cruiserweight belt. Cole won a unanimous decision, and, as Battle related, "the fight made the history books."

When asked about greatest fight Battle has ever worked, his response came without hesitation, "The Evander Holyfield–George Foreman fight." At that time, Holyfield was 25-0, a former Olympian, cruiserweight champion, and the unified heavyweight champion of the world. Foreman was 69-2 and a former world heavyweight champion, a hall of famer, and an Olympic gold medalist. He was also forty-two years old and undefeated in his return from a ten-year layoff.

Battle recalls the April 19, 1991, event in Atlantic City: "It was an eighty-million-dollar fight. Foreman surprised everyone by how competitively he fought. I probably could have stopped the fight in the seventh or eighth round, but I showed good judgment. I think George appreciated that." Evander Holyfield won a twelve-round unanimous decision. The fight, and Holyfield, Foreman, and Battle, made the cover of the April 29, 1991, issue of *Sports Illustrated*.

In his career, Battle worked many great boxing matches and officiated contests involving many great fighters. His last was a title fight involving Arturo Gatti. He was also third man in Arturo Gatti vs. Tracy Harris Patterson, Evander Holyfield vs. Alex Stewart, and Aaron Pryor vs. Gary Hinton. He refereed fights involving Jermain Taylor, Dariusz Michalczweski, Joe Calzaghe, Bernard Hopkins, Shane Mosley, Andrew Golota, Naseem Hamed, Terry Norris, Lennox Lewis, Meldrick Taylor, Buddy McGirt, Orlando Canizales, Myung-Woo Yuh, Mike Tyson, Jeff Fenech, Howard Davis, and Ray Mancini.

Battle is also proud of his involvement mentoring young men in boxing, especially Bernard Hopkins, the legendary great who became boxing's oldest champion, at forty-six years of age, in May 2011. "I knew Bernard Hopkins as a kid," he said. "He was involved in gang banging and the street life. He was from the Germantown area of Pennsylvania. I knew him as an amateur boxer, starting out. He had a lot of talent, but I told him he needed to get away from the street life. He and his brothers were always hanging out on corners, with other gang bangers. I would drive by, and pull up, and they were always planning something. I tried to guide him in the right direction, but he ended up getting incarcerated.

"At that time, I was volunteering my time to work as a referee in prison boxing matches. Bernard Hopkins was sent to Graterford," said Battle of the penitentiary where Hopkins was serving a five-year sentence for robbery. Battle refereed a fight involving Hopkins and spoke with him. Hopkins asked Battle to visit him. Battle did, occasionally putting some "money on his books," giving him commissary spending money. Battle mentored Hopkins, helped him get a job when he got out of prison, and provided him with advice. Bernard Hopkins never went back to prison; instead he became a champion, a role model, a future hall of famer, and an all-time great. Hopkins's brother and other childhood friends, however, went to prison and were murdered.

Battle faced a dilemma when he was selected by the IBF to be the referee for Hopkins's world title fight on April 29, 1995, against Segundo Mercado. He had previously been the referee for Hopkins's fights, but never for a bout of this magnitude. It was Hopkins's third try at a title—he lost a decision to Roy Jones Jr. in 1993 (a loss later avenged) and drew with Mercado in 1994. Despite their previous relationship, Battle accepted the assignment. He would not compromise himself, and he spoke to Hopkins before the fight to let him know there would be no favoritism. Hopkins likewise told Battle, "When we get into the trenches, you do what you have to do."

Hopkins won the title by a seventh-round technical knockout. Battle was an impartial official during the contest. The man who had stuck with and believed in Hopkins during his incarceration had officiated over his first world title win.

In June 2011, Bernard Hopkins was invited to come Harrisburg by the Pennsylvania State Senate to be honored after becoming the oldest champion in boxing history. In his speech, which can be seen on YouTube, Hopkins heaped praise on Battle for never giving up on him and for visiting him and mentoring him in prison.

As boxing commissioner, much of Battle's work today includes overseeing MMA, often thought to be replacing boxing as the premier combat sport. Battle himself has an honorary masters title in Ving Tsun Kung Fu and an honorary black belt in Song Do Kwan.

Battle tries to have his officials conduct themselves as he would have. He believes referees should be intimately familiar with the rules, especially rules surrounding fouls. Sometimes officials stop reviewing the rules. They then start to deviate from those rules, start interpreting them in their own manner, and eventually "make their own rules." Battle says, "Follow the rules, no problems."

He believes integrity is the key. He teaches officials to always act with integrity in training seminars he gives. "That is the most important trait," he says. "That deals with your character, your morals, and your upright-ness—and that is the goal to strive for."

3

Kenny Bayless

Multiple Referee of the Year award winner Kenny Bayless considers himself blessed and credits "the man upstairs" for his good fortune to referee the biggest boxing matches. He also thanks the Nevada Athletic Commission for allowing him to work those fights. Without taking anything away from the aforementioned, many would attribute Bayless's own work ethic, talent, and athletic ability to his success. He is among the most high-profile referees in boxing today, with a résumé that includes as many "super fights" as anyone in recent years.

Always an athlete, Bayless was an All-American runner at California State-Hayward in the 4x400-meter relay, which he ran with his twin brother, Kermit, who is now a California boxing judge. Kenny also ran the 400-meter dash, in which Kermit was a three time All-American. The 400-meter run is considered amongst the toughest athletic events, as it requires the speed of a sprinter along with the endurance and conditioning of a longer-distance runner.

Bayless grew up in Berkley, but left the Bay area after college and moved to Las Vegas to teach in 1972. Once there, Bayless became a regular spectator at local boxing events in the city. He had grown up watching the Tuesday night fights, the Pabst Blue Ribbon sponsored fights, and boxing on the *Wide World of Sports*. He was a huge Muhammad Ali fan in college.

The first opportunity Bayless had to work in boxing was at local Las Vegas shows as a glove man, working the equipment table. His initial goal was to judge boxing, so he began judging amateur contests. At the time, he had no desire to become a referee. He started to work with John Lehman, a boxing business veteran who worked with promoters and also did some work with the Nevada commission. Lehman referred Bayless to the commission as someone to whom they should give an opportunity—someone who worked hard and knew the sport.

Bayless's first break in the professional ranks, due in part to John Lehman, was as an inspector for the Nevada Athletic Commission. From 1985 to 1991, he worked many of the big fights in Nevada. Bayless can be frequently seen on ESPN Classic, in the corner of the ring, as an inspector for such fights as Michael Spinks vs. Larry Holmes I and II, Sugar Ray Leonard vs. Thomas Hearns II, Sugar Ray Leonard vs. "Marvelous" Marvin Hagler, Evander Holyfield vs. Michael Dokes, and numerous Mike Tyson title defenses. Spinks vs. Holmes I was 1985's upset of the year, according to *Ring* magazine; Spinks beat Holmes and became the first light heavyweight champion to ever win the world heavyweight title, ending Holmes's reign of twenty successful title defenses, second only to Joe Louis.

While serving as an inspector, Bayless continued to judge the amateurs, in hopes of eventually working professional fights. Noted professional boxing judge Jerry Roth suggested to Bayless that he should try to learn to referee. "He asked me why I wanted to be a judge," explained Bayless. "He told me to try reffing. He said, 'you are in pretty good shape, why not give it a try, what do you have to lose?'"

Legendary referee Richard Steele agreed to train him. "He told me, 'I can teach you,'" said Bayless. "He took me under his wing and mentored me." In the meantime, Bayless continued to work as an inspector in addition to refereeing and judging in amateur boxing matches, such as the Golden Gloves.

In 1991, Bayless became a professional boxing referee in Nevada, which is considered to be one of the most elite officiating positions due to the large amount of big fights in Las Vegas. On September 17, 1994, Bayless refereed his first world title fight—a 105-pound minimumweight contest featuring world champ and future Hall of Famer Ricardo Lopez that was held on the Julio Cesar Chavez vs. Meldrick Taylor II undercard.

Since then, boxing has taken Bayless around the world—he has been to Mexico on numerous occasions as well as Switzerland, Japan, China, the Philippines, and Thailand—and put him center ring in some of the biggest fights in history. He was the third man in the ring for such mega-fights as Manny Pacquiao vs. Shane Mosley, Floyd Mayweather Jr. vs. Shane Mosley, Manny Pacquiao vs. Miguel Cotto, Manny Pacquiao vs. Ricky Hatton, Antonio Margarito vs. Miguel Cotto I, Manny Pacquiao vs. Juan Manuel Marquez II, Floyd Mayweather Jr. vs. Oscar De La Hoya, Shane Mosley vs. Fernando Vargas II, Manny Pacquiao vs. Erik Morales II, Bernard Hopkins vs. Oscar De La Hoya, Roy Jones vs. Antonio Tarver I, and Erik Morales vs. Marco Antonio Barrera III. On October 11, 1996, he was the referee for Floyd Mayweather's professional debut after winning a bronze medal in the 1996 Summer Olympics. He has also worked fights involving Vitali Klitschko, Joel Casamayor, Eric Morel, Vernon Forrest, Julio Cesar Chavez, Paulie Ayala, and Terry Norris.

Even with all of his big fight experience, there are certain bouts that stand out in Bayless's mind. He cites Margarito vs. Cotto I as a "great fight," so much so that he attended their second fight at Madison Square Garden as a fan. "Seeing a fight at the Garden, as a fan, was on my 'bucket list,'" he stated. "Pacquiao vs. Hatton was also a great fight. The build-up of the fight dictates how big [the events] are," said Bayless. "Floyd Mayweather vs. Oscar De La Hoya was a big fight. But I treat them all the same. I have been blessed to work these fights, and that the Athletic Commission holds my work in high regard." He also indicated that Morales vs. Barrera III and Pacquiao vs. Morales II were "great fights, very entertaining." Bayless indicated that it was an honor to work the fights of Barrera, Johnny Tapia, and Julio Cesar Chavez, citing some of the retired fighters he has officiated. He marveled at what "great Mexican warriors" Barrera and Tapia were, and how they always put on a good show.

The Floyd Mayweather Jr. vs. Oscar De La Hoya fight on May 5, 2007, officiated by Bayless in Las Vegas, is listed by *Forbes* as the biggest pay-per-view fight of all time, with 2.4 million buys. It is said that after pay-per-view revenues were calculated, De La Hoya made $52 million and Mayweather $25 million. The fight also had a live gate, or paid attendance, of $19 million and sold out in three hours. Mayweather won the World Boxing Council light middleweight title with a twelve-round split decision over an aging De La Hoya, who had been a pro since winning the gold medal in the 1992 Olympics.

Bayless also considers himself fortunate in his personal and professional life outside boxing. Before he retired from teaching in 2007, Bayless had taught for thirty-five years, focusing on health and physical education. Twenty-nine of those years were spent teaching middle school. The last six were spent at a juvenile detention center. Bayless is a family man, married to his wife, Lynora, a wellness coach, for more than twenty-five years, with three grown sons, all former high school athletes, one of whom played professional basketball in Europe and South America.

Bayless remains an astute student of the sport of boxing—learning from all of the referees in Nevada. He also says he was fortunate to have a mentor like Richard Steele. Over the years, he has studied such noted third men as Davey Pearl, Joey Curtis, Carlos Padilla, Toby Gibson, Vic Drakulich, Russell Mora, Tony Weeks, Jay Nady, Mills Lane, Joe Cortez, and Robert Byrd. He carefully watches all fights, all fighters, and shares notes with other referees on fighters and their tendencies, especially in bouts involving lesser-known fighters. Reflecting the true educator he is, Bayless's philosophy on boxing is, "You are never too old to learn."

4

Robert Byrd

World Boxing Hall of Fame referee and decorated former police commander Robert Byrd is enjoying what few would consider to be a "traditional" retirement. While he may no longer be patrolling the streets as a member of the California Highway Patrol, he still works several jobs, and the accolades keep coming in for this Marine Corp veteran who has officiated more than a hundred title fights. His motto is "never fail because you were unprepared; give something back, and never forget who you are, what you are, and from whence you came."

Byrd grew up on the tough streets of Chicago's south side. After graduating from Dunbar High School, where he was a letterman in football and track and a member of the band, Byrd volunteered for the U.S. Marine Corps. While in the Marines, he saw action in the Cuban Missile Crisis and the initial stages of the Vietnam War. He was also a member of the Marine Corps boxing team, where he was a teammate of two other future Hall of Famers—legendary referee Richard Steele and future heavyweight champion Ken Norton, who is now in the World Boxing Hall of Fame and the International Boxing Hall of Fame. Byrd won the 139 pound title (light welterweight) while in the Marines.

After his active duty ended, Byrd joined the California State Police in 1966. "I joined the police and stayed out in California. It was the California

State Police then, but they merged with the California Highway Patrol in 1995." He enjoyed an incredible thirty-four year career that saw him rise to the rank of commander, becoming the first African American to be promoted above the rank of lieutenant in the history of the organization. Byrd retired from the California Highway Patrol in 2000. He also graduated from the Federal Bureau of Investigation's National Academy, which is a professional course of study for both national and international upper-level law enforcement management.

Byrd continued boxing into his police career. From 1976 to 1980 he fought in the California Police Olympics and won two gold medals, a silver, and a bronze. Upon his retirement from active participation as a boxer, he began his career as an official in California.

"In California, we had more boxing than any other state. They may not always have fights at the same level as in Nevada, but you do keep very busy, and I was happy," said Byrd of his time as a California boxing official.

"I had just retired from the police department. And I ran into Marc Ratner, from the Nevada commission, at a convention. Richard Steele had just retired [although he would come back again, and later retire]. When I heard that Richard was retiring, I joked to Ratner, just teasing, 'Now you will have room for me.' And he looked at me and asked, 'You would really consider moving here?' I thought about it, and could tell he was serious, and I said 'I would move here.' I came over to Nevada; I attended a commission meeting, and submitted my résumé. I met with Marc Ratner and Dr. Flip Homansky [a commission member in Nevada]. I came over as a judge, and about three months later, I slipped into refereeing."

Retirement has not slowed Byrd a bit. In addition to refereeing and judging boxing matches, he also works as an official for high school basketball and volleyball games, as well as security at both the MGM Grand and the Thomas Mack Center, home of University of Nevada, Las Vegas, Runnin' Rebels basketball team.

Byrd is half of one of combat sports' most prominent "power couples." He is married to Adalaide Byrd, a well-respected world-class boxing and mixed martial arts judge. Adalaide has also judged many of boxing's biggest matches, including Floyd Mayweather Jr. vs. Victor Ortiz, Wladimir Klitschko vs. David Haye, Manny Pacquiao vs. Miguel Cotto, Manny Pacquiao vs. Oscar De La Hoya, and Joe Calzaghe vs. Jeff Lacy. She is one of the few judges who does "double duty," judging both boxing and MMA. Adalaide is one of the world's most experienced MMA judges; she has worked numerous Ultimate Fighting Championship (UFC) events, including multiple title fights, and she frequently judges matches on the television show *The Ultimate Fighter*.

"We first met at the IBF convention, in 1996, in Toronto," related Byrd, on how he met his better half. "We met again the next year at the convention, and started to talk. The next five or six months we talked and eventually got to know each other quite well. We got married in 2001."

The Byrds do not work the same fights, with Adalaide judging and Robert refereeing. However, they are both very active on Las Vegas cards, often working on the same cards multiple times a month. "We have worked together in the Police Olympics [in California], where we are still officials."

Over the years, Byrd has been the third man in the ring for many very significant battles, including Miguel Cotto vs. Ricardo Mayorga, Wladimir Klitschko vs. Samuel Peter II, Chad Dawson vs. Antonio Tarver, Joshua Clottey vs. Zab Judah, Bernard Hopkins vs. Ronald "Winky" Wright, Robert Guerrero vs. Orlando Salido, Lamon Brewster vs. Wladimir Klitschko I, Philip Holiday vs. Jeff Fenech, Tony Lopez vs. Jorge Paez, and Tony Lopez vs. Rocky Lockridge I and II.

Additionally, Byrd has refereed bouts involving many of boxing's other top talents, including Glen Johnson, Joseph Agbeko, Adrien Broner, Julio Cesar Chavez Jr., Yuriorkis Gamboa, Tomasz Adamek, Jeff Lacy, Jose Luis Castillo, Nonito Donaire, Jhonny Gonzalez, Kelly Pavlik, Shane Mosley, Rafael Marquez, Marco Antonio Barrera, Juan Manuel Marquez, Mark Johnson, Ike Ibeabuchi, Iran Barkley, Antonio Margarito, Henry Maske, Humberto Gonzalez, Roger Mayweather, Orlando Canizales, Felix Trinidad, and George Foreman.

Not surprisingly, given Byrd's active schedule and track record, he is also one of boxing's most experienced judges. He has sat ringside for many title fights, including Roy Jones Jr. vs. Julio Cesar Gonzalez and Acelino

Frietas vs. Joel Casamayor. He was one of the three judges for the epic battle between defending World Boxing Organization (WBO) super bantamweight titlist Marco Antonio Barrera and former world champ and Olympic gold medalist Kennedy McKinney, which ended with a twelfth-round Barrera stoppage, but not before the fighters would combine for six knockdowns. The war was the first main event of the HBO boxing series *Boxing After Dark*, which featured slightly lesser known names and often lower weight fighters than HBO's *World Championship Boxing*. The idea was considered risky at the time, but the fight was an instant classic, and *Boxing After Dark* was a success and remains an HBO programming staple.

Another familiar name Byrd worked with was fighter . . . Robert Byrd! A 130-pound boxer from Texas, and no relation to the referee, Robert Byrd fought in California multiple times. In 1989, he participated in the Great Western Forum's super featherweight tournament. He made it to the semifinals of the tournament at the Forum, home of basketball's Los Angeles Lakers. Byrd was the referee in his contest with Edward "Pee Wee" Parker, who stopped him in the seventh round.

"At the end of the year, I got a W-2 from Forum boxing," said Byrd. "I opened it up and said, 'man, I know I didn't make that much from boxing at the Forum this year!'" Of course, what happened was a case of mistaken identity—Byrd had received both the boxer's and the referee's W-2 forms.

Byrd was elected to the World Boxing Hall of Fame in 2006, to the California Boxing Hall of Fame in 2005, and was recognized as one of the top ten referees in boxing by *The Ring* and *Boxing Illustrated* in 2001. He is also a member of the Screen Actors Guild, and has been involved in several movies. He was in the 2001 movie *Ali*, starring Will Smith. "I played Willie Reddick, who was Sonny Liston's manager," said Byrd of his role in *Ali*. "I also played a boxing judge in the movie *Rocky Balboa*. I was a consultant on the HBO movie *Don King: Only in America*."

To a young person who wants to be a boxer, the multifaceted Byrd offers this advice, "Be dedicated. Have the intestinal fortitude to do it. Not everyone is the most talented, but if you have the stomach, the heart, and are mentally tough, you can be a success—even though you might not be as talented."

As for those who look to become a boxing referee, Byrd stated, "Start out in the amateurs. Do your homework. Be patient. Not only in terms of years involved, but also your growth. If you screw up on a major stage, it hurts your career forever." Byrd pulled from his military and police experience when he said, "Work on your game—practice as you play. You need to be working on your craft. I am in the boxing gym six or seven times a month, working sparring matches."

Byrd stressed that becoming a referee is not just something one can decide to do overnight and be prepared for or successful. "You got to know the rules. If you don't know them, you can't apply them, or [know] when to apply them correctly." He reiterated the importance of the referee, the power he has, and how it must be used correctly and responsibly. "Keep focused—when you step in the ring, you have two lives in your hands. This is a tough sport. People can die in the ring and you can play a major part in that, or in someone getting hurt. Not always—things do happen. Maybe a fighter is not training, or is dehydrated, or was taking beatings in the gym. But you don't want an injury to happen because you are not prepared."

Byrd reflected on some of the lessons learned through experience, recalling "I was just starting out. It was in California. Some guy came to the fights, and was sitting right at ringside. And he kept yelling 'Stop the fight!' And I almost stopped the fight. I was nervous, I wanted to do right. I was asking myself during the round 'was that the commissioner?' Then I saw him yelling it between rounds, and I smiled and caught myself. For a minute I [had] questioned myself, and I could have had a career-wrecker. You have to distinguish the voices of your people, your commissioners, from the people in the crowd."

When asked about the most memorable fight that he had refereed, Byrd did not hesitate. "That would be my very first title fight. Tony Lopez and Rocky Lockridge," recalling the July 23, 1988, battle where Lopez dethroned defending champion Lockridge for the IBF junior lightweight title.

"There were about eighteen, nineteen thousand people there," recalled Byrd. "They packed the Arco Arena. Sacramento really hadn't had many boxing champions. There were some excellent boxers, but no champions. I remember standing in the ring before the fight. You know how they say 'there is electricity in the air?' Well, there really was electricity in the air. You could feel it. It was packed, and the fight was on national TV, for free. I looked around, and I said 'I'm here.' That was a great fight. It won the 1988 *The Ring* magazine Fight of the Year. They did it again, the next year. And both fighters, both camps, said 'we want Byrd.' So I got to referee that fight as well. For me, Lopez and Lockridge, that will always be my number one."

5

Frank Cappuccino

"Now both of you touch gloves . . . I leave it with you." With these words from referee Frank Cappuccino ending the pre-fight center ring instructions, so began perhaps the most exciting trilogy in boxing history—three fights and thirty rounds of non-stop fury between "Irish" Mickey Ward and Arturo "Thunder" Gatti.

And leave it to them he did. Cappuccino has always been known for letting fighters fight. He refereed the first, and perhaps the best, bout of the three between Ward and Gatti. Ward, who later gained Hollywood fame by being the subject of the Oscar-nominated movie *The Fighter*, won the first fight but lost the next two.

At various times during the bout, each boxer's cornerman wanted to stop the fight. Dickie Ecklund, the brother/trainer of Ward, and former two division champion/trainer of Gatti James "Buddy" McGirt both expressed that they did not want to see their fighters take too much punishment. But neither Gatti nor Ward wanted the fight stopped—neither had any quit in him. And the referee, Cappuccino, did not stop the fight either.

Gatti took violent punishment from Ward in the ninth round and was sent down by a brutal Ward body shot. Before the tenth round, Ward believed that Gatti's corner had stopped the fight, and began joyfully celebrating. "Fight ain't over, fight ain't over," Cappuccino admonished Ward, waving him back to the corner to resume the action. In a final round that typified the bout, Gatti stormed back to win the tenth, but lost a too-close-to-call fight.

The May 18, 2002, bout was an instant classic. Ward vs. Gatti I is listed as the number three fight of all time by *Men's Fitness* magazine and number four by *Time* magazine. It is perhaps the greatest non-title fight in boxing history.

It was an old-school, throwback fight refereed by an old-school, throwback referee. Throughout his career, Cappuccino gained a reputation for not interjecting himself in a boxing match, but he is proud that he "never got anyone badly hurt in the ring."

From a hardscrabble upbringing in the Italian section of south Philadelphia, Frank and his brother Vic, who went by the name of Vic Capcino, were both standout boxers. Frank started fighting at age four and had approximately 130 amateur bouts before turning pro. The original family name was Capcino, but was changed to Cappuccino when they emigrated from Italy and went through Ellis Island. Cappuccino went 6-0 as a pro, fighting until 1949. He recognizes that he was not as talented a fighter as Vic, who had a longer professional career, going 22-6. "Back in those days, you would fight for $75," said Cappuccino of his time as a pro, "but that was before paying the trainer, the second, and the cut man."

A self-made man, Cappuccino worked thirty-seven years as a supervisor for the Keebler Company and a sanitation inspector for the Philadelphia school district. He obtained his referee's license in 1958. He learned from the best, including all-time greats Zach Clayton, Ruby Goldstein, and Pete Tomasco. Cappuccino credits these referees with mentoring him and espousing the philosophy of not touching the fighters unless necessary and to stay under the television picture.

Cappuccino prides himself on his honesty and placing fighters first. Growing up in Philadelphia, he stated he knew of the "guys from the mob," such as the notorious Frank "Blinky" Palermo and Paul "Frankie" Carbo, of Murder, Inc., who were also involved in boxing management. "I never worked with anyone, no one could buy me, no one could tell me what to do. I only had problems with one guy, one guy who tried to get me—and

I told him to get away from me or I was going to break his jaw," said the 5'6 ½" Cappuccino. He never had problems with that individual again and said the man respected him.

Cappuccino's refereeing career ended in 2008 after he had a knee replacement. "I had to stop, my movement wasn't there," he said. "I was thinking more about the pain in my knee than the fights."

But what a career it was. A member of both the Pennsylvania and the New Jersey Boxing Hall of Fame, Cappuccino officiated over the biggest fight in the storied history of Atlantic City boxing—the June 27, 1988, bout between Mike Tyson and Michael Spinks. Tyson and Spinks were both undefeated, with the seemingly indestructible twenty-one-year-old Tyson having won the International Boxing Federation, World Boxing Association, and World Boxing Council titles. Spinks held the "lineal" title, as he was considered by many as the true heavyweight champion. Spinks had twice beaten recognized champion Larry Holmes, who was previously undefeated at 48-0 with twenty successful heavyweight title defenses. Spinks was also a former light heavyweight champion and Olympic gold medalist. Tyson continued his path of devastation, taking out Spinks in ninety-one seconds. Amazingly, Tyson earned $19.5 million, Spinks was paid $13.2 million, and Cappuccino received only $1,300.

"That was the biggest night in Atlantic City boxing. Everyone was there, and wanted to talk boxing with me—Jack Nicholson, Charlie Sheen, all the stars," said Cappuccino. "Everyone said when they saw the fight, that Michael Spinks was scared. They said he looked scared. He didn't look scared. I had done his fights before. That is how he always looked."

"Now, Alex Stewart, he was scared. His lip was quivering when I went up to him before the fight," said Cappuccino of Stewart, a heavyweight who had started his career in Tyson-esque fashion with twenty-four consecutive knockouts but whom Tyson knocked out at 2:27 in the first round of their December 8, 1990, matchup.

Cappuccino was the referee or judge in ninety-three world title fights. He officiated in thirty-eight countries, including eight fights in Italy, which meant a lot to him as an Italian-American. He appeared as a boxing referee in the movie *Rocky V*, starring Sylvester Stallone. He was the referee in

Lennox Lewis's knockout over Shannon Briggs for the WBC Heavyweight title in 1998 and a judge in the 1983 light heavyweight title unification bout where Michael Spinks won a fifteen round decision over Dwight Muhammad Qawi.

Cappuccino's refereeing résumé reads like a "who's who" of boxing greats. If they passed through Philadelphia or Atlantic City (and back in the 1980s and 1990s, most did), chances are high that Cappuccino worked their bouts. This includes Tyson (six times), Spinks, Ward and Gatti, Zab Judah, Bernard Hopkins, Kostya Tszyu, Johnny Tapia, Lennox Lewis, James Toney, Hector Camacho, Michael Moorer, Pernell Whitaker, Riddick Bowe, Bobby Czyz, Tim Witherspoon, Meldrick Taylor, Julio Cesar Chavez, Donovan "Razor" Ruddock, Gerry Cooney, Frankie Randall, Mark Breland, Marlon Starling, Simon Brown, Maurice Blocker, Mike McCallum, Vinny Pazienza, Marvin Hagler, Pinklon Thomas, Tommy Morrison (a *Rocky V* costar), Iran Barkley, Rocky Lockridge, Roger Mayweather, Matthew Saad Muhammad, Mike Rossman, Frank "the Animal" Fletcher, and Bennie Briscoe. Of all the fighters whom Cappuccino officiated, the one who impressed him the most was another hard-knock, honest, and no-frills fighter who worked that much harder than everyone else to achieve greatness—Marvin Hagler. "I like the way he handled himself in the ring, and outside of the ring. He was a great fighter, and he was a straight fighter, not nasty. He carried himself like a fighter. He was a true champion," said Cappuccino of his fellow southpaw, all-time middleweight great, and Hall of Famer.

Cappuccino earned his reputation as a referee who never got a fighter badly hurt in the ring and stayed out of the action unless necessary. He says he was able to pull this off by taking control in the dressing room, with the pre-fight instructions. "I never liked to touch the fighters in the ring. I once went six fights without touching a fighter. I used voice control during a fight. In the pre-fight instructions, I would be a son of a bitch. I would read them the riot act. I would let him know where I came from. I would tell them 'don't jam me,' in a way they appreciated, and that would stay in the back of their head when they were fighting.

"I didn't care what the guy had done in the past, what his reputation for fighting was. As long as he fought the way he should be fighting in this fight," reflected Cappuccino, "we had no problems during the fight." There was a calculated method to his tactics that made him one of boxing's all-time great referees. Cappuccino also spoke with pride when he said that during the fight he "treated everyone like the champ."

Eddie Cotton

Security guards formed a diagonal line inside the ring to keep Lennox Lewis and Mike Tyson from starting their heavyweight championship fight before the bell rang. At a press conference several months earlier Tyson had bitten Lewis in the thigh and threatened to eat his unborn children, and tensions were still running high at fight time.

The phalanx of guards was a riveting spectacle, but that night in Memphis, with Eddie Cotton as referee, the extra security was totally superfluous. Cotton had learned years earlier how to handle inflammatory situations in a boxing ring by refereeing fights in New Jersey's toughest maximum-security prisons. Hard cases with an attitude didn't faze him.

"I did fights in New Jersey prisons from 1984–1992," Cotton told the *New York Times* in a May 29, 2002, article by Dave Anderson titled, "The Most Important Referee." "There were only four referees approved by the state to do amateur bouts in the prisons, and we were paid $25 for an entire night of boxing. Refereeing at these prisons really prepared me for the professional game."

For the inmates, fighting for the prison championship was like fighting for a world title. "You were told not to stop these fights," recalled Cotton in his interview. "'Let 'em get knocked out,' we were told. The fights were supposed to be under amateur rules, but 'Stop,' 'Box,' and 'Break' didn't carry much weight in the penitentiary when a lot of those guys were serving a double-life sentence."

Born in California, Eddie and his family moved to Paterson, New Jersey, when he was three years old. As a boy he listened to fights on the radio with his father, Eddie Sr. (not the cagey 1960s light heavyweight contender, but a decent amateur fighter and one-time navy boxing champion). Eddie and his dad also watched the weekly "Gillette Cavalcade of Sports" fight series on television, and he got hooked on the sport, seeing championship matches involving the likes of Sugar Ray Robinson and Archie Moore.

In Paterson, Cotton attended Eastside High School (which years later become the focal point of the movie *Lean on Me*, starring Morgan Freeman). Afterward he was drafted into the army and served about three years in Germany. To get out of mess duty, Eddie volunteered to referee basketball and football games on the post, and when he returned home from active duty he continued as a referee on the gridiron and in amateur hoops.

Elected to the Paterson City Council in 1980, Cotton eventually became chief of staff to the mayor. One year at a Fourth of July celebration amateur fights were on the bill. "I enjoyed officiating sports, and I had always wanted to try being a boxing referee," Cotton stated. "I approached Eddie Johnson, who was a referee, and asked if I could work one of the fights.

"The first bout I worked was between two 65-pound kids in a three round contest with one-minute rounds. I was hooked, and worked the next twelve years in the amateurs throughout New Jersey and also in the state penitentiaries that had boxing programs, like Rahway in Trenton," said Cotton. "I did this until I received my professional referee's license in 1992."

New Jersey boxing commissioner Larry Hazzard knew of Cotton's work in the amateurs and steered him into the pro game. "Larry and referees like Joe Cortez, Robert Byrd, and Richard Steele mentored me early," he said. "It was Larry who instilled in me the importance of making sure that every decision I made in the ring was backed up by the rulebook. You don't ever invent something in there."

Cotton's first pro job was a single preliminary fight on a card in Atlantic City. It was a one-fight-at-a-time learning process. Within a few years

Cotton was working main events and regional title fights, mostly in the then–boxing hotbed of Atlantic City.

The hotbed got downright combustible on December 14, 1996, when the much-anticipated rematch between heavyweights Riddick Bowe and Andrew Golota was held in Atlantic City. Their first fight, on July 11, 1996, at Madison Square Garden, ended when Golota was disqualified in the seventh round after repeatedly fouling the former world champion. A full-scale riot ensued, first between the fighter's entourages and then the crowd. The eyes of the boxing world were on Atlantic City for the rematch.

Cotton, who had previously refereed two of Golota's fights, was assigned to work the "Foul Pole's" rematch with Bowe. Joe Pasquale, a judge of several undercard bouts that night, overheard Hazzard comment as Cotton entered the ring, "For this fight that is the best ref in the world."

Golota picked up where he'd left off in the Garden, and in the second round Cotton took a point from him for an intentional head butt. A series of low blows resulted in further deductions in round four. But Golota was still winning the fight, having scored legitimate knockdowns in the second and fifth rounds. He held a commanding lead in the ninth when he again started aiming low. After repeated warnings and more point deductions, Golota whacked Bowe with an uppercut below the belt, sending him to the canvas in agony. Cotton immediately stopped the fight and disqualified the Polish fighter. This time there was no riot, only unqualified praise for the no-nonsense referee.

Over the next few years Cotton refereed bouts involving more big names in the heavyweight division, including Michael Grant, Lamon Brewster, Oleg Maskaev, and Hasim Rahman. He also worked the final two bouts of George Foreman's remarkable career, against Lou Savarese and Shannon Briggs.

"George was a great person to deal with before and during his bouts, a true gentleman," recalled Cotton. "He always stood up between rounds of his fights, which most fighters do not do. He graciously accepted defeat in his final bout against Briggs, although many observers thought he deserved the victory."

It was two weeks before Lennox Lewis was to defend his heavyweight title against Mike Tyson on June 8, 2002, when Cotton received a telegram from the World Boxing Council appointing him as referee of the mega-fight at the Pyramid in Memphis. Hazzard, brought in as a special consultant for the fight, told the *New York Times* in "The Most Important Referee," "Eddie is deserving of any big fight. He has the background. His size is a factor, absolutely. You need size and strength to deal with Lewis and Tyson."

On account of the unprecedented security detail in the ring, which was responsible for keeping the openly hostile fighters apart until the first bell, Cotton gave Tyson and Lewis their instructions separately in their dressing rooms.

"We're starting from scratch with a clean slate," he told Tyson. "All the stuff in the past is out the window. I expect you to abide by the rules and I expect a good clean fight and for you to obey my commands," said Cotton when interviewed by Robert Ecksel for www.thesweetscience.com on August 3, 2011, in "The Third Man: Eddie Cotton."

The challenger respected Cotton's authority. "He was a complete gentleman during our meeting," Cotton recalled in the article. "He said, 'Yes, sir.'"

The atmosphere in Lewis's dressing room was very tense. "When I arrived there Lennox was sitting on the couch wearing sunglasses and he did not rise to greet me as Tyson had," recollected Cotton. "Lewis's trainer, Emanuel Steward, spoke for the champion. 'Eddie we are glad you're the referee for this fight,' he said. 'You have the size and experience of working with heavyweights and have always done a good job. But we are concerned about clinches. If there's a clinch we want it broken up, we don't want the boxers fighting out of it or for there to be a lull before you break the action.'

"I speculated that Lewis's team may have been concerned that Tyson would either bite him or bend his arm in a clinch, or commit some other foul if the clinches weren't immediately broken," said Cotton.

The boxing commissioner agreed with Lewis's team and instructed Cotton to separate the fighters immediately when they clinched.

In the match itself, "Tyson actually fought a clean fight, and it was Lewis who clinched and held and pushed Tyson down several times during the contest," recalled Cotton. "I finally took a point from Lewis in the fourth round, because he had previously been warned about it. When Lewis pushed Tyson down in the fourth he then took a swing at him from behind

Tyson's back and missed. If he hadn't missed, who knows what might've erupted."

Lewis knocked out Tyson in the eighth round. Each fighter grossed over $20 million. Cotton was paid $8,000 for his work, a seeming pittance next to the boxers' pay, but actually an excellent payday for a referee. For world championship fights a referee is usually paid somewhere between $1,800 and $5,500 and on a standard pro card he will net just a few hundred dollars. Referees are independent contractors, and when there is a title at stake, their pay depends on the size of the purses paid to the boxers competing.

But Cotton didn't get into it for the money. "Refereeing is a labor of love that has brought me to several countries around the world," he said. "I'm proud to have worked an event like Tyson-Lewis and actually I would have done it for free."

Not long after that fight, Cotton attended the annual WBC convention, held in Tokyo. At 6'5" tall and approximately 240 pounds, he towered over his Japanese hosts and almost everybody else. But somehow as the roll call of convention participants was recited on the first day of the convention his name was not heard, as it was left off the roster. That changed when a member of the Japanese Boxing Commission stood up, pointed at him and excitedly announced, "There's Eddie Cotton, the referee for the Lennox Lewis and Mike Tyson fight! I want him for our next title fight in Japan!" A few weeks later, Cotton was back in Japan to referee a WBC title fight.

Cotton is in favor of the standing eight count rule, which has now been eliminated by most boxing commissions. "I realize most people are not in favor of this rule," he stated, "and when I was only a spectator years ago I didn't like it myself. But as a referee the standing eight count gives me the opportunity to make an assessment of a struggling boxer to see if he is able to continue in a bout. I would only recommend using it once per bout. But if still in force it would eliminate some controversy from bouts that maybe are stopped too soon."

When a fighter gets up from a knockdown, Cotton doesn't ask him if he wants to continue boxing. "I may ask, 'Where are you?' or another question intended to jar his memory and let me know if he has his faculties," he said. "I also will ask him to come forward to me so I can make a determination about his coordination and evaluate whether he is in condition to continue fighting."

Cotton has officiated at two title defenses in Germany by current heavyweight champion Wladimir Klitschko. The one in which Klitschko stopped Ruslan Chagaev in nine rounds in Gelsenkirchen on June 20, 2009, drew sixty-one thousand people to Veltins Arena, the largest crowd to attend a fight in Germany since national idol Max Schmeling's heyday.

Cotton recently retired as director of operations for the Paterson Housing Authority, where his responsibilities included dealing with more than fifteen hundred family units and problems faced by tenants regarding maintenance issues and eviction notices. Now he fills his days working in real estate and improving his golf game—and staying prepared for the next refereeing assignment that comes his way.

Vic Drakulich

Reno attorney Vic Drakulich, a professional boxing referee since 1986, got his start in boxing while working his friend Mike Martino's corner in the late 1970s. That led Drakulich, who had excelled in high school football as an honorable mention all-state defensive end, to start down the path to a career as one of boxing's best referees. The gentlemanly Drakulich has worked almost fifty world title fights and has distinguished himself in the legal arena as well.

Drakulich, whose license plate reads "3RD MAN," is proud to have been in the ring for three Manny Pacquiao title fights—Pacquiao vs. David Diaz, Pacquiao vs. Erik Morales III, and Pacquiao vs. Jorge Solis. He officiated over the 2011 junior welter title unification match with Amir Khan and Zab Judah and the 2010 rematch of the ESPN 2009 fight of the year between Juan Manuel Marquez and Juan Diaz. He has also refereed title fights featuring Shane Mosley, Jorge Arce, Tim Bradley, and Devon Alexander. In 2010, Drakulich was named the referee of the year by the World Boxing Council. He has earned as much as $5,500 for refereeing title fights, a large amount for an official, but which pales in comparison to what he has made as an attorney.

Drakulich is semi-retired from an impressive legal career that has seen him win several multimillion dollar cases, including a $22.4-million-dollar verdict that was later reduced to $6 million in a 1988 case. This success has enabled him to focus on boxing and spend time with his family. As a highly experienced litigator with extensive criminal and civil experience, Drakulich still works with other attorneys, often younger lawyers, if a case is going to trial. One attorney that he has worked with both in and outside the ring is former professional boxer Joey Gilbert—a three-time NCAA boxing champion and a contestant on the television show *The Contender*—who retired in 2010 with a 20-3 record. Drakulich refereed several of Gilbert's fights, including his 2009 twelve-round decision loss to local rival Jesse Brinkley, which was a major event in Reno.

While studying at the University of Pacific McGeorge School of Law, Drakulich's constitutional law professor was future U.S. Supreme Court justice Anthony Kennedy. After graduating in 1975, he began his legal career as a public defender. At the time, his wife, Linda, his brother, and his boxing mentor, Mike Martino, were all juvenile probation officers. Today, Linda is a school guidance counselor. The couple, who have been married for more than thirty years, have three successful daughters, Jessica, Alyse, and Dionne.

Drakulich grew up watching boxing. He never competitively boxed but would go to the local YMCA in Reno and spar. He was also a member of the high school football team, which his father, Duke Drakulich, coached. Working Mike Martino's corner first led Drakulich to judging and then to refereeing amateur fights, from 1981 to 1986, until he received a professional license. While Drakulich does not regularly referee amateur fights anymore, he still works collegiate bouts, as well as the United States Air Force Academy's "Wing Open" Championships, which he has refereed for more than fifteen years.

While Drakulich has worked numerous high profile fights involving some of the world's best, both in Las Vegas and across the nation, some are especially memorable. "I did four Oscar De La Hoya fights, three for world titles," he recalled. "Oscar De La Hoya really stands out. A great fighter, and such a gentleman." Drakulich was the referee for De La Hoya's 2001 win over Javier Castillejo to earn the WBC light middleweight title, his seventh round technical knockout over Luis Ramon "Yori Boy" Campas in 2003 for the World Boxing Association (WBA) and WBC 154 pound titles, and his close 2004 win over Felix Sturm to gain the WBO middleweight title.

"Manny Pacquiao and David Diaz is a fight that really stands out to me," said Drakulich of the June 28, 2008, contest for Diaz's WBC light-weight title, held at Mandalay Bay in Las Vegas. Pacquiao won by a ninth round technical knockout after delivering a brutal beating to the "never say die" Diaz, one of the true warriors of the sport. Pacquiao was moving up to 135 pounds after having won titles at 112, 122, 126, and 130 pounds.

"This was a rough and tumble fight. They were two excellent boxers," Drakulich continued. "At the end of the fight, Pacquiao landed a punch that sent Diaz down face first, and I waved off the fight. Diaz was on the ground, had rolled over on to his back, and was still groggy. I was attending to Diaz, and waiting for the doctor to take a look at him. Pacquiao came over to shake his hand. I remember Diaz's face lit up, and everyone forgot everything and they just touched hands. I actually had to wave Pacquiao off so the doctor could get at Diaz. What a great show of sportsmanship between two great sportsmen."

To a young person who desires to become a boxer, Drakulich offers the following advice: "I highly recommend it, but make sure to do your homework, go to a qualified gym, and work with a qualified instructor. In Reno, we have a coach named Greg Rice, who coached at Nevada-Reno, and he really teaches solid fundamentals. That is very important."

Drakulich suggests that someone who is interested in becoming a referee should contact his or her local amateur organization. "Sign up, and work your way up the ranks. In time, when the official has gained experience, he should contact his local professional commission, and inquire about becoming a pro referee."

His approach to working a fight is to remain calm and levelheaded. Drakulich believes in learning about a fighter's style. He believes that in a fight with rules infractions, sometimes the best way to control the fight is to administer a point deduction. To explain, he cites a fight he refereed—the November 12, 2011, WBO light welterweight title fight between champion Tim Bradley and former world champ Joel Casamayor, on the undercard of the Manny Pacquiao vs. Juan Manuel Marquez III fight at the MGM Grand in Las Vegas. During the match, Casamayor had been holding to the point where a deduction was merited. In the fourth round, after repeated warnings, Drakulich took a point away from Casamayor. "That ended the holding," said Drakulich, "and the rest of the fight was a clean one," and remained so until Bradley scored an eighth-round stoppage.

In the 2003 article "Reno's Drakulich Stands Out as Man in Middle of Ring," in the *Reno Gazette-Journal*, Drakulich spoke about his duties in the ring: "It's very tough. You have competing factors. You have a guy who has dedicated his life to boxing. This fight is important to him and his family. At the same time, his physical and mental well-being is more important. [Knowing when to stop a fight] comes from years and years of doing this— not too soon, not doing it too late. You have to do what you think is right. You live with the consequences. I've never had much criticism from my calls [to stop fights]. I've been very fortunate."

Similar to the way he approached his legal career, the cerebral Drakulich takes an analytical and educational approach to boxing. He watches the sport as much as he can. "I always analyze it, analyze the officials, and never stop learning," he said. "I believe that in each fight, the boxer, the officials, the referees—we all learn."

8

Benjy Esteves

Benjy Esteves's house is filled with photos of family members and items that represent his strong Catholic faith, but nothing to indicate that he is a top professional boxing referee. He has worked major title fights all over the world, some of them involving such megastars as Floyd Mayweather, Shane Mosley, "Prince" Naseem Hamed, and Arturo Gatti.

"Refereeing is a major part of my life, but it comes after God and my family and friends," he explained, "and when people enter my house I want them to see that."

In the entertainment room in his basement, Esteves has his collection of boxing photos and the punching bag on which he exercises to stay in top form. The name Francisco "Paco" Rodriguez is written on the bag in tribute to the boxer, who passed away after a 2009 fight Esteves refereed. A boxer's death is the worst thing that can happen to a referee.

"The fight between Teon Kennedy and Francisco Rodriguez took place at the Blue Horizon in Philadelphia," recalled Esteves. "It was scheduled for twelve rounds, for the USBA title. It was a competitive bout and both boxers gave and took punishment throughout the contest. I asked the corner of Francisco Rodriguez several times in the bout if he was all right to continue, and I also brought in the ringside physician for his opinion."

After Esteves stopped the fight in the tenth round he walked the coherent Rodriguez back to his corner. Moments later, Rodriguez slumped over on his stool and slipped into unconsciousness. He was rushed to the hospital, and Esteves followed along to pray for the fallen fighter. Rodriguez passed away two days later. No one was critical of how Esteves handled the bout, but the fighter's death will always be with him.

"I have thought about it many times and I don't think I would have done anything differently as the referee in the fight," said Esteves. "I keep a picture of Francisco in my workout area. May God rest his soul."

Born in Milwaukee, Wisconsin, Esteves and his family moved to Manhattan's tough Hell's Kitchen neighborhood when he was three years old. Their mother, Irene Nieves Esteves, raised Benjy and his brother, Norberto. "My mother was my role model," Esteves said. "She got my brother and I involved in sports at a young age to keep us busy and away from gangs and drugs. She also emphasized the virtues of physical fitness, honesty, and integrity. She was always a very giving person with a solid work ethic. She worked long hours in a factory and always preached to my brother and me that it is more important to try to be nice than to try to be important."

Norberto Esteves did some amateur boxing, and their uncle, Victor Melendez, was a promising featherweight in New York in the late 1960s, losing only to Ismael Laguna and Carlos Teo Cruz, both of whom went on to win world titles. Melendez also fought Mike Cortez, whose brother, Joe, would become one of the game's top referees. Joe also became a friend and mentor of Esteves after he started refereeing on the professional level.

When the boxing bug finally bit Esteves, he was too old to put on the gloves, so he set his sights instead on becoming a referee. Breaking in was no easy process. "I started by calling the office of *The Ring* magazine, then located in Manhattan," he recalled. "That led me to Bruce Silverglade, who owned Gleason's Gym and also ran the amateur program in New York. Eventually, I befriended amateur boxing official Frankie Martinez, who mentored me and taught me so much about refereeing. Frankie was also from Hell's Kitchen and we just clicked, he mentored me and called me a natural.

"Frankie taught me never to make remarks to anyone about any of the boxers before a bout, to not make any predictions, and to always be on time and ready to go to work. He also told me to continually work on my craft and never get complacent, and to be aware that there is always an opportunity to improve."

Gleason's Gym, on 31st Street in New York City, became one of Esteves's hangouts. There he attended seminars on refereeing and had the opportunity to observe 1940s ring legends like Rocky Graziano and Jake LaMotta hanging around the gym and watch such modern ones as Roberto Duran and Wilfred Benitez training for fights.

Luis Rivera was another early mentor. Rivera, a former pro fighter who once boxed against Vito Antuofermo, had refereed several of Mike Tyson's bouts, including his professional debut. "Luis took me to the gym and put me in a ring," Esteves recollected. "He wanted to see me move around and critique my style. The first advice he gave me was, 'When the fighters start moving slow, you pick up the pace. When the fighters start moving fast, you slow down.'"

For thirteen years, while learning the referee's trade in the New York amateur ranks, Esteves worked as a process server. He delivered complaints and summonses to people in some of the Big Apple's toughest areas, and though he treated everyone he served with dignity and respect, it was not always reciprocated. He found himself staring down the barrel of many a gun, and New Jersey boxing judge and Esteves admirer Joe Pasquale is probably only half-kidding when he says that Esteves's career as a process server "probably explains the great footwork he exhibits in the ring today."

After a few years as an amateur referee Esteves was elected chief of officials in New York State, becoming responsible for training all the amateur officials there. He donated his time to the amateur game in New York for seven years before relocating to New Jersey and a less hazardous day job in the accounts receivable department at IBM. At the time Esteves had no thought of advancing into the professional ring, but after New Jersey boxing commissioner Larry Hazzard saw him work some amateur bouts he recruited Esteves to join the pro ranks.

"I refereed my first professional fight on July 30, 1992, in Stanhope," Esteves recalled. "Joe Gatti, the older brother of Arturo, won by a first-round knockout."

Esteves never went back to the amateurs. "Although I also loved refereeing amateur boxing," he stated, "I felt that since I'd made it as a referee in professional boxing, if I continued to referee in the amateurs I would be taking someone's spot in amateurs who might have dreams of becoming a professional boxing referee."

Esteves had the opportunity to learn from some of the greatest referees in the world who lived on the East Coast, including Joe Cortez, Randy Neumann, Frank Cappuccino, Rudy Battle, Arthur Mercante Sr., and Steve Smoger. "I had access to all of them when I broke in and I took full advantage of it," said Esteves. "Joe Cortez relocated to Las Vegas years ago, but I still talk to him frequently and ask his advice."

After just a year in the pros, Esteves had the chance to referee main events. His first world title fight was on November 18, 1995, in Atlantic City, when Felix Trinidad defended his IBF welterweight championship with a fourth-round knockout of Larry Barnes. He was also the referee when Kostya Tszyu suffered his first career defeat to Vince Phillips, and for Arturo Gatti's slugfest victory over Gabriel Ruelas.

On December 19, 1997, Esteves was selected to referee the American debut of British sensation "Prince" Naseem Hamed at Madison Square Garden. The former world champion and local hero Kevin Kelley was in the other corner for the WBO featherweight title bout, televised live on HBO.

"When I found out that afternoon that I would do the main event," recalled Esteves, "the first thing I did was head up to the cheap seats, or nosebleed section, where I always sat when I was just a young fan of the sport and could barely afford to get into the Garden. It put everything into perspective as I sat there and reflected on how far I had come in boxing. There is nothing like working at the Garden."

That night he visited the fighters' dressing rooms to go over the rules. "Usually, most boxers are very respectful when we do that," said Esteves. But it was different with the British boxer. "As I was reviewing the rules, Hamed interrupted me. 'All I want to know is if you can count to ten!' he said very abrasively. I knew he was trying to intimidate me and I just ignored him. You do your best to keep everything professional, not personal. I always remember what Rudy Battle told me long ago: 'You are not fighting these guys, you are refereeing them.'"

The crowd at Madison Square Garden was in a frenzy during Hamed's ten minute walk to the ring. The bout lived up to the hype, and both men visited the canvas a few times before Esteves stopped it in the fourth round to save Kelley from further punishment.

Since then Esteves has refereed title fights in Argentina, Russia, Italy, and Germany, among other international locales. He has also worked major East Coast bouts including Felix Trinidad vs. Pernell Whitaker and Miguel Cotto vs. "Sugar" Shane Mosley.

When IBO light heavyweight champion Antonio Tarver defended his title against ring legend Bernard Hopkins on June 10, 2006, in Atlantic City, Tarver and his handlers approached Esteves, the referee that night, concerned about Hopkins's tendency to hit his opponents on the hips. "The Tarver camp brought it up, so I had to address it," said Esteves. "Hopkins is a consummate professional and I have a lot of respect for him. Bernard will take whatever you give him. I told Hopkins that I would not judge him on past performances but I would be watching him. Everything in that fight worked out fine.

"A referee cannot focus all his attention on just one of the boxers," Esteves continued. "There are two fighters in there and the referee has to be neutral. I tell the boxers I referee I will give them what I expect from them—a professional effort."

Of course, it isn't just the fighters who have to be watched. They have handlers who will try anything to give their guy an advantage. Sometimes their methods are ingenious. Esteves recalled refereeing a preliminary fight years ago in Atlantic City in which one of the boxers incurred a severe cut on his forehead when he banged heads with the other fighter. "I had the ringside doctor come in to check it between rounds," he said, "because it looked really bad. But the doc and I were both amazed to find when we got to the corner that the bleeding had stopped. The guy with the cut not only continued but went on to win the fight. I found out later that in the corner his trainer had pushed the boxer's hair into the cut and covered it with Vaseline so it looked very natural. It was a great job and I commended him as he did nothing illegal."

The referee's job, said Esteves, "is to keep the boxers safe and also maintain the integrity of the sport. In the ring, my mind is on the fighters and I'm also concerned with my positioning in the ring and making sure I'm always moving and limiting myself from blocking the judges' view. My focus is on the boxers; I need to be prepared for many things, like a mouthpiece falling out and which corner to take it to, as well as looking for cuts, butts, or other fouls."

Maintaining strict professionalism is a requirement outside the ring, as well. "When I see boxers I know on the street or at a social function, I say hello and keep it very brief," he said. "I try not to have conversations with any of the fighters outside the ropes. It could give someone the opening to say something if it appears that I'm overfriendly with a boxer whose fight I end up refereeing. Also, I don't schmooze with promoters. If I get an assignment locally or out of town, I stay clear of the promoter. I deal with the commission or my supervisor if any issues come up."

Esteves's high profile in boxing won him the chance to appear as a referee in the 2009 romantic film comedy *The Rebound*, starring Catherine Zeta-Jones and Justin Bartha. "It's about a journalist who goes to different sporting events," Esteves said, "one of which is a boxing match. I got the part through then–New York boxing commissioner Ron Scott Stevens, who played the fight announcer in the movie."

One of Esteves's remaining goals before he leaves boxing is to referee a bout in Puerto Rico, the land of his heritage. "Even if it is just a preliminary bout, it would mean so much to me."

He and his family live in Sayreville, New Jersey, less than an hour's drive from New York City. In his spare time, Esteves details cars and often donates time to a local food pantry and speaks with kids about the virtues of living a clean life.

Esteves and his wife, Nelsie, have been married more than thirty years and have two sons, Julian and Benjamin III. Sayreville is a peaceable town, but Esteves doesn't leave the house windows open at night and always attaches "The Club" to the steering wheel after parking his car outside his home.

"Growing up in Hell's Kitchen," he said, "old habits die hard."

9

Howard John Foster

S ome referees are known for a famous catchphrase. Others display
certain flair around the ring, or bear a famous family name that
resonates in the sport. Then there are those renowned simply for
their competence—for being among the best in the business. Howard
Foster fits that bill.

The veteran of nearly fifty world title bouts has impressed boxing officials around the world with his professionalism and commitment to the
sport he has loved since he was a boy. A construction builder from
Doncaster in South Yorkshire, England, Foster has refereed bouts in his
native country, as well as in Ireland, Australia, Germany, Italy, Finland, the
Ukraine, the United States, and South Africa.

"My first memory of the sport is listening to Cassius Clay/Ali fights on
the radio and watching his fights with Henry Cooper," recalled Foster.
Cooper was the 1960s British Commonwealth and European champion,
whose calling card was a big left hook celebrated by his legions of fans as
"'Enry's 'Ammer."

In Cooper's 1963 fight with Clay, the 'Ammer pounded Clay to the
canvas at the end of the fourth round, and many still maintain that it was
trickery by Angelo Dundee in Clay's corner in cutting Clay's gloves and
buying time that enabled him to go on to stop Cooper on cuts in the next

round. After Clay became heavyweight champion and changed his name to Muhammad Ali, the two met again in a 1966 world heavyweight title match, which Ali won in six rounds. Though he didn't ever win the title, in 2000 Cooper (who passed away in 2011) became the first and only boxer knighted by the Queen of England.

While he only had two makeshift fights as a schoolboy, Foster admired the referees he grew up watching. Even as an adult he talked so much about them that his wife, Debbie, finally told him he ought to think about getting into that line of work himself. He applied to the British Boxing Board of Control (BBBC) and began the long, slow process of climbing the ladder.

"To be a referee in Britain, you have to first sit for an interview with your area council of the BBBC," Foster explained. "If you are successful, you are then asked to start going to shows and scoring the bouts. In Britain, all referees score the fights. There are no judges for all bouts up to the British title level.

"If you are successful with your scoring, you then get invited to appear before the referees' committee for a further interview on rules and regulations. If you are successful in this, you are then asked to do trial fights in the ring, and then if you pass your trial fights you are given your Class B license, which allows you to referee fights up to eight rounds.

"All this takes about two years," Foster said. "You are assessed throughout your refereeing, and if you are considered competent enough you will be upgraded to a Class A referee, which allows you to referee up to 10 three-minute round fights."

Class A referees undergo further evaluation, and those who pass muster are elevated to a "Star Class" status, which allows them to officiate national title bouts and accept overseas assignments. "It is a very long process, but well worth it," said Foster. He received his Class B license in 1997, allowing him to work professional fights. By January 2000, he was upgraded from Class B to Class A. Foster achieved Star Class status just over five years after he began, earning top honors in January 2003. It was a swift ascent through the ranks, rivaled only by that of the legendary Harry Gibbs.

Foster's total professionalism in the ring was evident from the start. "I recall seeing him at his first appointment as a qualified referee and was suitably impressed and had the pleasure of telling him so," stated Mickey Vann, one of Britain's all-time great third men in the ring, in an interview. "I look for confidence in a referee's performance. I want to see pride in his appearance and a good person outside of the ring. Howard had all these attributes and still does."

International boxing judge and author David Hudson stated, "Howard refereed a couple bouts I judged in South Africa in 2011. He worked so seamlessly that you realized you were witnessing one of the best referees in action. He had total control of the ring but allowed the fighters to fight. He's also a first-class human being, and treats everyone with respect."

Phil Austin—a judge, referee and supervisor for the IBO who lives in Australia—seconded that motion in an interview with the authors. "We are always very keen to have him work over here," he said. "The British system is the best in the world, bar none, and Howard is a top graduate of that system. What I especially like about Howard—a very unassuming guy—is his quiet confidence in his own ability. He does what has to be done, when it needs to be done. He misses very, very few fouls and gives a fighter every chance, but when it is time to pull the plug he does not hesitate."

For Foster, the hardest call a referee has is when to stop a fight. "There is a very fine line," he said, "but I always say it is better to stop it a little early than a little too late. I would be mortified if a fighter was to die or get permanently injured when I was the third man in the ring. I always keep a close eye on a boxer who starts to look a little weary or is starting to take a beating. I'm never afraid to stop a fight."

It was Foster himself who ended up taking a beating after he stopped the 2009 European Boxing Union light welterweight title fight between Giuseppe Lauri and Juho Tolppola in Helsinki, Finland, and awarded it to Lauri on a foul.

Even after having two points taken away, Tolppola continued to hold and hit and rabbit punch Lauri. Erik Schmidt of www.boxingnews24.com reported that in the tenth round, Tolppola landed a right hand to the back of Lauri's head just as Foster was in the process of breaking the two fighters. At that point, Foster had seen enough and immediately disqualified

Tolppola at 2:10 of the tenth. Seconds after the stoppage, a chunky-looking man emerged from Tolppola's corner and went after the referee and nailed him with a right hand to the midsection before he was tackled by one of the boxing officials in the ring, who pinned the irate man to the canvas.

The assailant turned out to be Tolppola's father. After he was subdued, spectators started throwing coins at the ring; one hit Foster in the chest. As security guards led him out of the arena, Foster was punched in the face by a fan.

"In boxing, you take the good with the bad," he said.

There has been plenty of the good. In May of 2008, he refereed the Ricky Hatton vs. Juan Lazcano fight in a Manchester stadium before a crowd of almost sixty thousand. Hatton won a lopsided twelve-round decision in what Foster recalled as "one of the greatest occasions in recent British boxing history."

Seven months later, Foster refereed the IBO cruiserweight title bout between Danny "The Green Machine" Green and Roy Jones Jr. at Acer Arena in Sydney, Australia. Once considered boxing's pound-for-pound best, Jones was well past his prime at this point and was stopped in the first round.

Foster also worked Green's subsequent title defense against B. J. Flores in Mt. Claremont, Australia, which the popular native son won by decision. One of the most memorable championship bouts he has worked, said Foster, was the rubber match between Clinton Woods and Glen Johnson for the IBF light heavyweight title in Lancashire, England. Woods won the September 2, 2006, fight by split decision.

Foster's ironclad control of the action in the ring came in for high praise after the 2006 rematch between British heavyweights Matt Skelton and Danny Williams. Foul tactics on both sides had marred their first bout, but that didn't happen the second time around with Foster in charge. "Foster never allowed it to degenerate into the unseemly bout of biffs and butts rough-house of their previous encounter, which went down as one of the dirtiest fights of the decade," wrote Alan Hubbard in *The Independent*. "Foster stopped most of the aberrations before they started, at one stage pulling both men apart and warning: 'I can throw you both out—I don't care.'" Accolades are fine, but "I'm my biggest critic and I'm always trying to improve," said the "Star Class" referee whose star is still on the rise.

10

Frank Garza

Lincoln Park, Michigan, referee Frank Garza has worked for Buckeye Pipeline for thirty-seven years as a station operator. Yet he views refereeing boxing as a profession, not a hobby, and said he is "quick to scold those involved in boxing who view their duties otherwise." Garza's philosophy on refereeing incorporates what he terms "the four C's"—compassion, concern, courteousness, and the most important, common sense. He believes that all referees must have an abundance of these qualities.

Garza grew up in Delphos, Ohio, and has always been a boxing fan. He is the son of hard-working parents from the Rio Grande Valley. He fondly remembers watching the Gillette and Pabst Blue Ribbon sponsored fights as well as weekend fights on ABC's *Wide World of Sports*. He said that he briefly worked out at the Lima, Ohio, boxing club before moving to Michigan. Once he relocated he worked out regularly, trained at boxing gyms, and later became a coach.

Garza was first licensed as a professional judge in 1984 and as a professional referee in 1986. He judged many important fights in the 1980s, and began getting regular work as a referee in 1992, after working his way up through the Golden Gloves and the amateurs, according to a 2000 article in the *Detroit Free Press*. Garza indicates that he got his big break when the

International Boxing Federation (IBF) split from the WBA, which gave some newer officials a chance to work bigger fights. "When the WBA split and the IBF was formed, a lot of the senior officials did not want to go. The IBF gave us the opportunity to work the big fights. Now, I am a WBC official, and as far as I'm concerned, that's the ultimate."

Perhaps the biggest event that Garza worked, and the fight that put him on the international boxing map, was the October 20, 2000, bout between former world champion Mike Tyson and Andrew Golota at The Palace in Auburn Hills, Michigan. The contest featured two awesome talents whose careers and reputations had been marred by unsportsmanlike conduct, fouls, legal issues, and erratic behavior.

Tyson was only four fights removed from his infamous "ear biting" incident in his loss to Evander Holyfield in 1997. He had done little to redeem his reputation in the interim—he claimed to have tried to break Francois Botha's arm in a stoppage victory, and his bout with Orlin Norris was ruled a "no contest" when Tyson hit him and knocked him down after the bell, causing Norris to injure his knee. In the bout prior to Golota, Tyson fought fringe contender Lou Savarese and stopped him in thirty-eight seconds. Tyson hurt Savarese with almost anything he threw and knocked him down fifteen seconds into the fight. In a frightening display, the referee, the highly experienced John Coyle, attempted to stop the bout, but Tyson continued to rain punches in, pulling down the referee with a left hook. After the fight, a charged-up Tyson went on a rant when interviewed and threatened to eat champion Lennox Lewis's children.

Andrew Golota was best known for being disqualified twice for repeated low blows against former world heavyweight champion Riddick Bowe. He also froze and was knocked out in one round by champ Lennox Lewis and quit a bout he was winning against prospect Michael Grant. These incidents overshadowed the former Olympic bronze medalist's incredible talents, and the fact he was beating Bowe and Grant when the fights were stopped.

Tyson vs. Golota was a match that appealed not only to the boxing enthusiast but also to the general public. It was promoted as a match between boxing's "bad boys," a must-see spectacle where anything could happen.

Many non-boxing insiders were surprised by the selection of Garza to referee the Tyson vs. Golota fight, as they were used to seeing Tyson in the ring with higher-profile Nevada and New Jersey referees. An October 13, 2000, Associated Press article by Ed Schuyler Jr. was titled "Frank 'Who' to Referee Tyson-Golota Fight." *Sports Illustrated* did a feature on Garza before the fight, and with a nod to the fighters' not-so-clean reputations, author Rick Reilly said, "Next to Joan Rivers's makeup man or Bobby Knight's career counselor, Garza has the worst job in America. He's the poor bastard who will be trapped inside the ring with these two animals for as many as 12 rounds of malice at the Palace of Auburn Hills." Quick to accept a challenge in a high-profile assignment, Garza saw this as a chance for the fighters to dispel their negative images. In pre-fight instructions, he made it clear that all of the sins of the past would be forgiven if the fighters fought cleanly. He let Tyson and Golota know this was a chance to redeem themselves. "I told each fighter before the fight that they could absolve themselves of everything they had done in the past in the ring. This was a new career for them."

Once the fight began, Tyson knocked Golota down in the first round, and Garza marveled at the chin of Golota, who got up and kept fighting after a punch that would have taken out most other fighters. "He could take tremendous punishment, because there was no way he should have got up after that punch," he said. "And Golota came back and fought competitively after."

After the second round, however, Golota refused to go to his corner, pushing away Garza, as well as his trainers, all of whom tried to get him to sit on the stool and get ready for round three. "He told me he quit when he was walking around," said Garza. "I tried to give him a chance, and let his corner know he had until the next round started." When Golota refused to come out for the next round, Garza was left with no choice other than to stop the fight and award it to Tyson. As Golota left the ring, he was showered with boos and pelted with garbage and beer. The fight's result was later changed from a technical knockout to a third-round "no contest" when Tyson tested positive for marijuana.

Garza is introspective about the way Tyson vs. Golota was promoted, "There was PR all over the world that was trying to contact me beforehand.

And the fight was promoted as a spectacle. I didn't want to disgrace box-ing. It was promoted like, 'something bad can happen.' And while the fight went on, they fought very cleanly. We kept something crazy from happen-ing. I got calls from all over afterwards, from Jose Suliaman [the president of the WBC] and Marc Ratner [then the executive director of the Nevada State Athletic Commission, now the vice president of regulatory affairs for the Ultimate Fighting Championship], telling me that I did a great job, and that was the cleanest they had ever seen Tyson or Golota fight."

In 1996, Tommy "the Duke" Morrison was a well-known heavyweight contender and former WBO heavyweight champion. He was coming off of a bad one-sided stoppage loss to Lennox Lewis, but the former star of *Rocky V* still had a big name, a big punch, and had signed a lucrative contract with promoter Don King. An eventual bout with Mike Tyson was under discussion. Before his first tune-up fight of the contract, scheduled for February 10, 1996, against journeyman Arthur Weathers; however, Morrison tested positive for HIV. The fight was cancelled. Later that year, on November 3, 1996, in Chiba, Japan, Morrison had a fight on a George Foreman undercard and Garza agreed to be the referee. It was one of the only times that a fighter known to be HIV positive was allowed to fight.

The rules for this fight were different—there was an agreement that if either fighter were cut, the fight would be stopped, and the bout would go to the scorecards. The fight ended with Morrison stopping Marcus Rhode in round one. Garza indicated that he donated the money that he made from the fight to AIDS research.

Garza states that the reason he was selected to officiate the Morrison vs. Rhode fight goes back to a convention that he had attended prior to the match. Garza had participated in a conference where a doctor spoke of the dangers of AIDS and boxing, and told the group assembled about all the things that needed to be done, including mandatory testing of fight-ers. He objected that the doctors themselves were not being tested. "[At the time] we didn't know everything about HIV and AIDS," he reflected. "Who knows if Morrison would have gotten AIDS? Who knows if AIDS could be transmitted in the ring? I felt I needed to make myself aware of what could happen."

Garza has had the opportunity to work many major fights involving top fighters. He refereed the January 29, 2011, WBO/WBC junior welterweight title unification match between Timothy Bradley and Devon Alexander in the Silverdome in Pontiac, Michigan, on HBO's *World Championship Boxing*. He refereed the Carl Froch vs. Arthur Abraham fight in 2011 in Showtime's "Super Six World Boxing Classic" super middleweight tournament and judged in another bout in the same tournament, the 2010 bout between Andre Dirrell vs. Arthur Abraham. He has been the third man for Jermain Taylor vs. Ronald "Winky" Wright and Floyd Mayweather Jr. vs. Phillip N'dou, as well as fights involving Jhonny Gonzalez, Adrien Broner, Saul Alvarez, Kelly Pavlik, James Toney, Mark "Too Sharp" Johnson, Jeff Lacy, Erik Morales, Oba Carr, Roger Mayweather, Krzystzstof Wlodarczyk, and Oleg Maskaev. He has also officiated matches featuring some of the world's best women boxers, including Mary Jo Sanders (daughter of Detroit Lions football great Charlie Sanders), Christy Martin, and Mia St. John.

Garza cites Floyd Mayweather Jr., Saul "Canelo" Alvarez, and Mike Tyson as the most memorable boxers he has refereed. He states that Mayweather is the most talented, that Mike Tyson had a larger-than-life persona, and that the young Canelo has incredible popularity and charisma.

Officiating boxing is not Garza's only passion. For the past twenty years he has been a sports writer for Hispanic newspapers in the Detroit area. He has also authored an English-language article on sports for *Latino*, a newspaper in the Detroit area, for the last ten years. Garza writes about all sports, including boxing.

Garza stated that he tries to remain modest about his ring accomplishments, and to keep everything in perspective. Several years back, *The Ring* magazine named Garza the number six best referee in the world. Shortly afterward, he was in Canada and ran into former contender George Chuvalo, known for his fights with Muhammad Ali, George Foreman, and Joe Frazier, as well as his legendary chin and ability to absorb seemingly superhuman doses of punishment. Garza wanted to meet Chuvalo and to shake his hand. The two were introduced and someone mentioned to

Chuvalo that Garza had been named as the sixth best referee in the world by *The Ring*. Garza said that Chuvalo looked at him, grinned, and stated, "Mr. Garza, when you get to number one, call me."

11

Wayne Kelly

Wayne Kelly's mind wandered as he leaned back against a turnbuckle before the world heavyweight title unification fight on February 23, 2008, in Madison Square Garden between Wladimir Klitschko and Sultan Ibragimov.

Kelly looked around the packed Garden and thought, *I am refereeing a world heavyweight championship fight at Madison Square Garden. I am blessed. This will be something that will be with me the rest of my life.*

The road to that moment was a long one. Kelly had boxed as an amateur and had seven professional bouts. But that was a tiptoe through the tulips next to his military service in the Vietnam War. He was called to active duty at eighteen. "The Army put me through a grueling training program where the main objective was to turn myself and others into efficient and motivated combat-ready soldiers with a healthy desire to kill," he said. "The whole process took only five months in 1967—two months of boot camp and three months of basic training. Within days of being released from basic training, I found myself in the jungles of Vietnam with an M16 rifle. Upon arrival, I asked my platoon leader, 'What is it like here?' He responded, 'If you have a business in Vietnam and a house in hell, sell your business and go home.'"

For Kelly, the war was a crash course in maturity and survival. "For the soldiers, it was the uncomplaining acceptance of unendurable conditions," he stated. "And the soldier did accept the unendurable."

After serving ten months in the jungles of Vietnam, Kelly was sent to Australia for some rest and relaxation. There he visited some pubs and surfed at Bondi Beach. Little did he know then that he would return to Australia more than forty years later to referee a world title bout.

When Kelly returned to combat action in Vietnam, he was shot in battle and received a Purple Heart. His physical wounds healed, but thirty years later, he was treated for post-traumatic stress disorder (PTSD).

"I went back to Vietnam in 2000, on advice that a return trip might be therapeutic," he stated in an interview with the authors. "At a bar in Quinon I started speaking with a Vietnamese man. We exchanged a few rounds of beers and turned out that the man was also a boxing fan. I told him I was now a referee, but as we got into things I started talking about my tour of duty during the war. His face registered shock, and he told me that he also fought in the Vietnam War with the North Vietnamese Army. We found out that we had both been involved in a firefight in Bong Son. We had tried to kill each other over thirty years prior! We hugged and toasted each other's nation and then toasted to world peace."

When he was eight years old, Kelly's grandfather introduced him to boxing. "Harlem" Eddie Kelly was a successful pro fighter in New York who'd fought boxing legends the likes of Benny Leonard and Mickey Walker in his lengthy professional career. After learning the basics from his grandfather, Kelly was hooked and requested boxing gloves from his mother for his ninth birthday.

Kelly went on to have about thirty amateur bouts and won the Third Army light heavyweight title. Then he went to real war.

After returning from Vietnam, he resumed boxing. "I was a much better gym fighter than professional fighter," Kelly said. "I often sparred with light heavyweight contender 'Irish' Bobby Cassidy, and he convinced me to give professional boxing a try and acted as my cornerman. I won more than I lost, fighting mostly in Long Island City, New York."

Once Kelly hung up the gloves he decided to stay in the sport and refereed amateur boxing in New York for the next ten years. But he couldn't break into professional refereeing. He contacted the New York Athletic

Commission several times, and he also wrote letters asking for a tryout, but he never got an answer. His luck finally changed in 1988 when then commissioner Randy Gordon got in touch with him. Kelly's first assignment was a four-round bout at Brooklyn's Gleason's Arena. Within a few years, Kelly was refereeing main events in New York featuring world-class boxers Michael Dokes, Kevin Kelley, and Merqui Sosa.

On February 6, 1993, Riddick Bowe defended his world heavyweight title against Michael Dokes at Madison Square Garden. In a major crossroads bout on the undercard, Ray Mercer faced veteran trial-horse Jesse Ferguson for a big payday and a title shot against Bowe, if he won impressively. Kelly worked the Mercer vs. Ferguson fight and later found himself at the center of a huge controversy.

Mercer came in that night at highest weight of his career, and what looked like an easy night's work for him on paper instead turned into one of the biggest sports stories of the year—Mercer was thoroughly out-boxed by the fighter known as "Boogieman" and lost a ten-round decision. Afterward it was alleged that during the bout Mercer actually offered Ferguson a one-hundred-thousand-dollar bribe to take a dive. Mercer was formally charged with attempted bribery and went to trial. Kelly testified in court about what he heard during the fight.

"It's not uncommon for fighters to talk in the ring," he said, "and it's not against the rules. There was a decent amount of holding and talking going on during that fight, but they had their mouthpieces in and the conversation was mumbled. On the witness stand I told them the truth based on what I saw and heard."

Mercer was acquitted. Kelly was commended for his work both in the ring and the courtroom.

Kelly refereed several of Arturo Gatti's major bouts, including the one in which the exciting Gatti won the IBF junior lightweight title by beating Tracy Harris Patterson in the Garden on December 15, 1995. But it was Gatti's war with Wilson Rodriguez a year later that taught Kelly to always expect the unexpected.

"My research before the fight indicated that Rodriguez would come out boxing and counterpunching," stated Kelly, "but instead he came out firing, trying to knock out Gatti. I watch as much boxing as possible and study other referees on how they handle situations in the ring. I also try to get as much information on each boxer as I can before the fight. Some referees don't want to know anything about the fighters they will be refereeing but I like to know as much as possible."

One of the first lessons Wayne received was from his friend Al Gavin, one of boxing's legendary cutmen. Gavin worked the corner of a fighter in one of the first pro fights Kelly refereed. "Every few minutes, Gavin starts yelling from the corner, 'Hey, he's hitting my guys in the balls!' I never saw it happen, but because of all his yelling I started looking for the low blows," said Kelly. "Round after round, Gavin continued shouting about low blows. After the fight, when I told Al that I didn't see any low blows, he smiled at me and said, 'I got you, didn't I? There weren't any low blows.' Fortunately, it didn't affect the way that I refereed the bout, but Gavin did get in my head a bit and it taught me to trust my own judgment. From then on I took the approach, 'If I don't see it, it didn't happen.'"

Gavin later coached Kelly's son, Ryan, as an amateur, and Kelly's friendship with Gavin continued until Gavin died from a stroke in 2004.

Kelly was the referee in the first infamous fight between former heavyweight champion Riddick Bowe and then-undefeated Polish contender Andrew Golota on July 11, 1996, at Madison Square Garden. Dubbed "The Foul Pole" on account of his questionable tactics in the ring, Golota lived up to his reputation that night.

"I warned Golota three times for hitting low before I started deducting points," recalled Kelly to his former commission chairman Randy Gordon on the boxing website The Sweet Science on July 19, 2011. "He kept punching low and after the third point deduction, I told Golota, 'One more low blow and you are taking a shower!' He looked and me and indicated that he understood. Then he went right back out and drilled Bowe with another left hook below the belt. Bowe clutched his groin and fell to the canvas. I had no option but to disqualify Golota in the seventh round."

As Golota was standing in his corner, a Bowe handler rushed over and smashed a cell phone on the head of the disqualified fighter. Within minutes, chairs and other objects were being hurled around the Garden by rioting spectators. The fight was broadcast on HBO, and commentator George Foreman pleaded unsuccessfully with the crowd to calm down. New York City mayor Rudy Giuliani was rushed from his ringside seat to safety in one of the dressing rooms and remained there for more than an hour. The *Wall Street Journal* included the incident on its list of "Seven of History's Most Terrifying Sports Riots," and the bout was featured on HBO's award winning documentary series *Legendary Nights*.

As chaos engulfed the Garden, Kelly remained right at ring center. "I planned to stay in the ring," he said. "One of the security guards wanted to assist me out of the ring but my job wasn't done yet. It's my job to police the ring. I was concerned for my associates with the commission and my friends in the crowd, but I wasn't concerned about my own safety. Was I scared? No way. I've been shot more times than a rap star!" quipped Kelly to Randy Gordon in the article "Irish Wayne Kelly: He May Just be Boxing's Best Ref."

Among his favorite perks of the job are traveling all over the world and meeting celebrities who come to the fights. After one bout at Madison Square Garden, John F. Kennedy Jr. approached Kelly. "We spoke for some time. He was really a fight fan and had several questions for me on the specifics of refereeing. We had a lengthy and very enjoyable conversation."

It's a testimony to the respect Kelly has earned as a referee that he was called at the last minute to work the heavyweight title fight between Wladimir Klitschko and Chris Byrd on April 22, 2006, in Mannheim, Germany. The fighters' camps couldn't agree on a referee until Kelly's name was brought up. Just forty-eight hours before the fight (won by Klitschko on a seventh-round stoppage) Kelly hopped on a plane for Germany.

Kelly is always willing to assist young referees, lending his time and expertise to those eager to perfect their craft.

"Wayne has been a great help in my career as a referee," stated Charlie Fitch, a referee based in Rochester, New York. "He always gives me honest advice, and my association with him has improved my refereeing abilities. He's my favorite referee in boxing and I think he's among the top five in the world of the past twenty years or more. From my perspective his work is equal to that of Hall of Fame referees Arthur Mercante Sr., Larry Hazzard Sr., Joe Cortez, and Stanley Christodoulou.

"What I like about Wayne as a referee is he lets the fighters fight, and he has excellent judgment on knowing when to stop a fight," Fitch continued. "He doesn't intrude on the action, but is present when needed. That excellent judgment is what separates the world-class referees from everybody else. Wayne has kind of flown under the radar in my opinion. Part of that comes from the fact he is not at all a self-promoter. Once his work is done as a referee, give Wayne a cold beverage, some friends around him, and someone to flirt with, and he's happy as can be."

Fitch first met Kelly on September 27, 2003, in Buffalo, New York. The occasion was Fitch's very first assignment on a televised fight card. Eighteen thousand loud fans were there to cheer for their local hero, "Baby" Joe Mesi, in his heavyweight fight with DaVarryl Williamson on HBO's *Boxing After Dark* series. Fitch was assigned to work the televised undercard fight between Juan Carlos Gomez and Sinan Samil Sam, and was nervously sitting in the officials' dressing room beforehand doing some last-minute cramming.

"I had my head buried in my notes and was going over the rules for about the thousandth time," he recollected, "when suddenly the papers were ripped out of my hand and a booming voice declared, 'If you don't know these rules by now, you will never know them!' I looked up and there stood Wayne Kelly with my notes crumbled in his fist.

"I'd seen him on television working many of the biggest fights held over the last 10 years, with fighters like Roy Jones and Oscar De La Hoya. Now my guts twisted and I thought, *Great, Charlie! Way to make a good first impression on one of the world's best referees!* But then he cracked a big smile and told me to relax. That was exactly what I needed to hear. I knew those rules backwards and forwards. What I needed was to be calmed down, and that's what Wayne did in his unconventional way." Kelly has a different favorite memory of that night. Watching Fitch work in the ring, he thought Fitch's pants seemed a trifle baggier than necessary.

"I later found out," said Kelly, "that when Charlie picked up his pants from the dry cleaner on his way to the arena that night, they not only gave him the wrong pants, but they gave him pants that actually belonged to a woman! The poor guy ended up making his HBO debut wearing a pair of ladies pants!"

Kelly is retired from his full-time career in social work in the Services for the Aging division for the Town of Hempstead in New York. Fitch credits Kelly's career as a counselor for much of his success as a referee.

"He cares deeply about other people. I suspect that his social work background/mentality has been a major factor in Wayne's ability to balance the safety of the fighters with the sport's high demands and expectations for violence when he makes his decisions in the ring," explained Fitch. "I know other world-class referees whose full-time occupations reflect a broader social conscience. Some have backgrounds in the military, police work, the fire department, or the ambulance service, and that seems to be a common theme among the best referees."

Kelly works out regularly and teaches boxing to amateurs when not spending quality time with his daughter, Jackie, a schoolteacher, and son, Ryan, who followed his dad into the social work field.

Kelly's philosophy on life is simple and positive: "Toughness and compassion can go together. Treat the underdog with kindness and respect. Live simply and love generously. Keep your hands up, keep punching and keep living!"

POSTSCRIPT: On February 1, 2012, Wayne Kelly passed away from a heart attack at the far-too-young age of sixty-three. He will be remembered for his work as a referee, but far more importantly for being a man of honor and integrity. He is survived by his loving children. His service in the armed forces and social work will never be forgotten.

In a tribute, esteemed writer Thomas Hauser wrote, in his article "Wayne Kelly (1948–2012)" on www.thesweetscience.com, "Wayne Kelly was a class act and one of the many people who do their part to make boxing a great sport. He knew that the fighters, not the referee, were the story. When giving instructions before a bout, he never called attention to himself by uttering a signature phrase or doing anything else to grab the spotlight. He had a smile and kind word for everyone he met and was always willing to offer advice to young referees who were learning their craft.

"He was also a terrific referee; a blue-collar guy who got in the ring and did what he was supposed to do. He had great positioning and great judgment. He didn't stop fights too soon and he didn't let them go on too long. The boxing community could always count on Wayne Kelly to do his job right."

He will be missed.

12

Mills Lane

Wororld Boxing Hall of Famer Mills Lane is synonymous with big
time Las Vegas boxing from the 1970s to the late 1990s. When
you think of the big fights of that era, chances are good that the
stern, commanding, fit-looking Lane was center ring, signaling the start of
the bout at the end of the pre-fight instructions with his catchphrase, "Let's
get it on!" Lane was a renaissance man, a jack of all trades—judge, prosecutor, decorated boxer, and Marine Corps veteran—and he symbolized
excellence in officiating.

Lane was the third man in the ring in many of boxing's biggest and best
moments—true showcase fights and box-office blockbusters like Larry Holmes
vs. Gerry Cooney, Evander Holyfield vs. James "Buster" Douglas, Marvin
Hagler vs. John Mugabi, Larry Holmes vs. Ken Norton, Oscar De La Hoya
vs. Pernell Whitaker, and Mike Tyson's initial title-winning performance over
Trevor Berbick and his fight with Peter McNeeley after returning from prison.

It is said that when a referee does a great job, no one knows he is there,
and no one remembers who worked the fight. Many of the most vivid memories of Lane, however, were in moments of insanity in the ring—moments
where he was the calm in the eye of the storm. One such occasion was the
November 6, 1993, contest between IBF and WBA heavyweight champion
Riddick Bowe and former champ Evander Holyfield.

The fight, the second in a wonderful trilogy, is best remembered by the general public for the "Fan Man," an individual named James Miller who parachuted into the ring in the middle of the seventh round. The fight, held in the outdoor parking lot of Caesars Palace, was stopped for over fifteen minutes as security rushed to the ring, and Bowe's entourage beat Miller unconscious. Lost in the melee was the fight eventually resuming and Holyfield winning back his heavyweight title by a majority decision.

The year 1997 was a particularly wild one for fights involving Lane. On June 28, he was the third man in the rematch between heavyweight champ Evander Holyfield and Mike Tyson. The fight was an eagerly anticipated rematch of Holyfield's eleventh-round upset stoppage win over Tyson the previous year. The late Mitch Halpern was originally assigned to be the referee, but the Tyson camp objected, and Lane was named the third man instead. The fight set a record for all pay-per-view buys, which stood until broken by Floyd Mayweather vs. Oscar De La Hoya in 2007. It has been reported that Holyfield made $40 million, and Tyson made $35 million. Holyfield started out strong and rocked Tyson in the first. In the third, Tyson bit Holyfield's ear twice, the second time taking a chunk of Holyfield's flesh with him. Blood started spewing from Holyfield's ear, and Lane stepped in and disqualified Tyson. Lane's shirt, and the ring, was soaked in blood.

Only two weeks later, on July 12, 1997, Lane presided over a bizarre fight for the WBC heavyweight title, where Lennox Lewis retained his title in his first defense over previously undefeated Henry Akinwande at Caesars Tahoe in Stateline, Nevada, on HBO. Akinwande was disqualified for excessive and repeated holding, earning him the name "Hugging" Henry Akinwande.

Even more bizarre than the Lewis vs. Akinwande fight, however, were the circumstances under which Lewis won the WBC title, via technical knockout over Oliver McCall on February 7, 1997. McCall had previously won an upset knockout over Lewis to win the title but had since had numerous legal issues and a bad drug problem. McCall suffered an apparent breakdown during the fight, holding his hands down to his sides, taking punches from the hard-hitting Lewis, crying, and refusing to fight back. Lane stopped the fight, starting off a truly memorable 1997.

Lane retired after officiating a Thomas Hearns fight in 1998, doing what few do—retiring while on top. A household name after the Holyfield vs. Tyson fight, Lane went on to pursue other interests, which included starting a promotional company with Tony Holden and his two sons, Tommy and Terrance, called Let's Get it On Promotions. He also starred in his own television show, *Judge Mills Lane*, and his character likeness and voice were used in the MTV show *Celebrity Deathmatch*. In 1998 he wrote an autobiography, *Let's Get It On: Tough Talk from Boxing's Top Ref and Nevada's Most Outspoken Judge*.

Mills Lane was always a symbol of strength and commanded respect inside and outside the ring. He is a Marine Corps veteran. Lane was the 1960 NCAA welterweight champion, competing for the University of Nevada, Reno, and also competed in the Olympic Trials. He fought as a professional boxer from 1961 until 1967, and went 13-1. He became a lawyer, a prosecutor, and eventually served as the district attorney in Washoe County, Nevada (which includes Reno). He was elected judge in Washoe County in 1990, where he served until retiring in 1998.

During his career, Lane's résumé as a third man included many major fights in addition to the aforementioned ones. He refereed a bout between Muhammad Ali and light heavyweight champ and future Hall of Famer Bob Foster for the North American Boxing Federation heavyweight title. Lane's son, Tommy, points out that Ali, Foster, and Mills were all participants in the 1960 Olympic Boxing Trials. Ali, then known by his birth name of Cassius Clay, was an eventual Olympic gold medal winner. Ali put Foster down for the ten count in the eighth round to win the regional title.

Lane also refereed the following bouts: Livingstone Bramble vs. Ray Mancini II, Mike Tyson vs. James "Bonecrusher" Smith, Larry Holmes vs. Leon Spinks, Mike Tyson vs. Tony Tucker, Thomas Hearns vs. Juan Domingo Roldan, Evander Holyfield vs. Carlos De Leon, Hector Camacho vs. Ray Mancini, Pernell Whitaker vs. Azumah Nelson, Thomas Hearns vs. Virgil Hill, Mike Tyson vs. Donovan "Razor" Ruddock II, Evander Holyfield vs. Bert Cooper, Iran Barkley vs. Thomas Hearns II, Evander Holyfield vs. Larry Holmes, Terry Norris vs. Meldrick Taylor, Michael Carbajal vs. Humberto "Chiquita" Gonzalez I, Tommy Morrison vs. George Foreman,

Michael Moorer vs. Evander Holyfield I, Julio Cesar Chavez vs. Meldrick Taylor II, Lennox Lewis vs. Tommy Morrison, Mike Tyson vs. Frank Bruno II, Bernard Hopkins vs. Robert Allen I, Salvador Sanchez vs. Danny "Little Red" Lopez II, Michael Nunn vs. Frank Tate, Thomas Hearns vs. James Kinchen, Donald Curry vs. Milton McCrory, Larry Holmes vs. Carl "The Truth" Williams, Larry Holmes vs. Tim Witherspoon, Sugar Ray Leonard vs. Bruce Finch, Marvin Hagler vs. Vito Antuofermo I, Lupe Pintor vs. Carlos Zarate, and Earnie Shavers vs. Ken Norton.

In 2002, while enjoying the next phase of his career, the mighty Lane suffered a stroke, which has affected his ability to speak, but his mind remains as sharp as ever.

His son Tommy Lane, a Hofstra University graduate who lives in New York State after moving there with his family for the *Judge Mills Lane* show, is still involved in Let's Get it On Promotions. To date, their biggest event was the Jesse Brinkley vs. Joey Gilbert fight, held on February 14, 2009, at the Reno Events Center. The match featured two fighters from Northern Nevada—Brinkley is from Yerington and Gilbert is from Reno—both of whom were featured on season one of the television show *The Contender*. The fight was a war, with Brinkley winning a twelve round decision, flooring Gilbert and breaking his nose before a large and enthusiastic crowd.

"People came out who had never been to a boxing match before," said Tommy. "Both of the fighters had been on *The Contender*, and there were some articles about it in the newspaper the week of the fight. It was more like a high school football game, everyone local wanted to talk about it." Tommy said that Let's Get It On Promotions was started by his father "as something to do with his sons" and indicates that they are currently working on additional projects.

Tommy is a self-admitted boxing junkie who has watched most of his father's work in big fights. He related that his father appreciated working in all bouts, but that "his favorites were Salvador Sanchez vs. Danny 'Little Red' Lopez and Marvin Hagler vs. John Mugabi." The June 21, 1980, Sanchez vs. Lopez rematch at Caesars Palace was between two Hall of Famers for the WBC featherweight title, which Sanchez won by via technical knockout in round fourteen. Hagler vs. Mugabi was a shootout between middleweight champion Hagler and menacing undefeated challenger "the Beast" Mugabi, who came into the fight with a record of 25-0—25 knockouts. Hagler won via knockout in the eleventh. It was his final career victory. "My father said that the Lennox Lewis vs. Oliver McCall fight was the most bizarre, that and the 'Fan Man' fight. He always said that he didn't think Mike Tyson biting Evander Holyfield's ear was something that was premeditated, it was something that he did in the heat of battle," said Tommy.

"My father is doing ok. [The stroke] has affected his ability to speak. He can tell you what he wants, but it is difficult to have a conversation. The stroke has affected the right side of his body. His right arm is limp. But his mind is completely clear. Occasionally, he will go out to play poker at the casino, something he loves to do. He is a proud guy. He doesn't like people to see him the way he is. But his spirits are good. Basically, he leads a quiet, retired life," Tommy reports. He also indicates that his father is still instrumental in lending advice on their promotional efforts.

In 2006, a newly-built courthouse in Lane's hometown of Reno, Nevada, was named after him—the Mills B. Lane Justice Center. This Washoe County Court building houses the district attorney's office as well as several courtrooms and is a great source of pride for Mills Lane and his family. It is clear that Tommy has tremendous admiration for his father, and both father and son take great pride in Lane's reputation as a straight shooter. "How fair was my father? How much of a straight shooter was he? He did not know how to be dishonest," said Tommy. "When my father ran for judge, a lot of lawyers in town did not want a DA running for judge. They felt maybe he would not be fair, that he would favor the prosecution. But when my father was elected, he was compassionate as a judge. He was able to see the big picture, and do good for people. He was a fair guy."

Tommy said that it is a testament to his father that he was able to be an honest man in a sometimes dishonest business: "The boxing business is unbelievable. I could go on with stories. But my father is synonymous with honesty. He was a referee in a dirty business. He is a wonderful guy."

Lane put a premium on honesty, something he valued and passed on to his family. "The most trouble I ever got in from my dad was when I was ten years old," recalled Tommy. "I lied to him about whether I cleaned my room. I told him I had. And that was the worst punishment I ever got. My father was very angry. And I never lied to him again. He taught me that [lying] was the worst thing to do—I should be honest, straightforward. I have a loving father; he has always been fair, and honest."

POSTSCRIPT: In December 2012, Mills Lane was given boxing's ultimate honor, as he was elected to the International Boxing Hall of Fame.

13

Sparkle Lee

When a young Sparkle Lee attended an event as a spectator at Madison Square Garden for the first time, she couldn't believe all the punishment the contestants in the ring seemed to dish out and receive from her vantage point near the rafters. "Those guys really went at it and traded back in forth in a way I had never seen before," said Lee. "Finally, someone let me in on the truth—that professional wrestlers, although highly talented, were strictly in the entertainment business.

"Once I found out that professional wrestling was basically showbiz, I was done with it," she continued." Years later, I would find my true ring sport."

Sparkle, who was born and raised in Harlem and grew up one of sixteen children, took up boxing in 1982 along with her twin sister, Star. They started in a White Collar Boxing program at Gleason's Gym in Manhattan to improve their fitness level. Participants could compete in White Collar Boxing matches against other people who took up the sport for conditioning purposes and wanted to try actual competition. Five years later, Lee was sworn in as a police officer, working mainly out of the Bronx. She was encouraged to pursue a career as a boxer by the trainers at the gym, but as a mother and a cop she didn't have the time required for a successful career in the sweet science.

"Bruce Silverglade, the owner of Gleason's Gym, then recommended that I get involved as an official in amateur boxing," said Lee.

As one of New York's Finest, Lee did her share of refereeing in the streets. On one domestic dispute call in Harlem, she was confronted by a man twice her size. "He told me that he had just got out of jail for beating up a cop, and he doubted that I was going to stop him," she recalled in an interview.

"I'm not stupid, I'm not going to go in there fighting. I remained calm, got on my radio, and when a couple more cops came I said to the guy, 'Is that enough?'" she later explained to the *New York Daily News* in a May 15, 2011, article. "Being a cop, you have to use your mind and stay calm. If you get crazy, and they're already crazy, then something's going to happen. I want to go home the same way I came in." Lee worked as an amateur boxing judge for seven years before she started refereeing amateur contests. "When I started officiating in 1983, Mark Breland and Mike Tyson hadn't turned pro yet," she said. "I remember watching them at some of my initial amateur events."

Her debut as a referee was not a resounding success. "In my first amateur bout, the boxers kept punching right through my commands," she said. "I was frustrated and hard on myself after that match. But I just kept learning and trying to improve from there."

That meant working every show she could, including small smokers in tiny basements. On weekends when she wasn't working, Lee often rode a bus to Atlantic City to watch professional boxing. She became of a big fan of Larry Hazzard, who refereed many of the major bouts there at the time. "I truly admired his presence and footwork in the ring," she stated.

After fifteen years in the amateur trenches, in 1998 Lee became the first female to referee in the prestigious New York Golden Gloves tournament. "My family would ask why I continued to donate so much time to amateur boxing when there had never even been a female referee in the Golden Gloves," she said. "I have always had a lot of faith in God and a good work ethic, and felt it would pay off some day for me. It was an honor to be selected as the first woman to ever officiate in the New York Golden Gloves."

Three years earlier, women had been allowed to fight in the Golden Gloves for the first time, a change accompanied by lots of fanfare. But the debut of the tournament's first woman referee was more low-key, which was fine by Lee. "I was there to do a job—protect the boxers and enforce the rules," she said. "I wasn't interested in being in any spotlight."

Her obvious competence could not be denied, and eventually Lee was put in charge of all the amateur boxing officials in New York City, making assignments and delegating responsibilities.

Meanwhile, she continued to attend seminars with an eye to breaking into the pro ranks. In the mid-1990s, she applied for a referee's license with the state athletic commission. "I paid the seventy-five dollar application fee, and then-commissioner Randy Gordon took me to Gleason's Gym to evaluate my performance in the ring," Lee recalled. "I thought I was on my way, but then Randy Gordon lost his job as commissioner and my application sort of fell through the cracks. Then I considered becoming a boxing inspector, but a guy at the commission told me, 'Don't sell yourself short.' So I kept plugging away."

Whenever possible, she went to New Jersey to study the finer points of refereeing with world-class third man in the ring Benjy Esteves, who became a special mentor. Lee also avidly studied tapes of fights refereed by Joe Cortez and Larry Hazzard.

At the time, the only female referee of note in professional boxing was Gwen Adair, who had been working in California since 1980. In 1998, Adair became the first woman to referee a world title fight, a match for the International Boxing Federation's junior middleweight title between Pedro Ortega and Luis "Yory Boy" Campas in Tijuana, Mexico.

"She was the torch-bearer for us," stated Sparkle, who finally broke through the glass ceiling in 2001, when the New York commission issued her a license. In her pro boxing debut, she refereed two four-round bouts on a club show in Queens. "It was a memorable night," she recalled, "and my fights went off without a problem."

Lee continued to work prelims in New York, and was excited to get a call one day from Larry Hazzard, who had become the chairman of the New Jersey boxing commission. He said he was always looking for quality referees and urged Lee to apply for a license in the Garden State.

She did, and before long, Lee was handling main events on the Boardwalk in Atlantic City. On November 17, 2007, Lee arrived for a card at Borgata Hotel Casino figuring that she would work the undercard of the headline attraction—a regional title fight between hot prospect Abner Mares and Damian David Marchiano, which would be broadcast on HBO's *Boxing After Dark*. Instead, she got the call for the main event, which she handled with her usual aplomb (after notifying her family to make sure everybody tuned in for her TV debut).

Lee's first international assignment was the 2008 IBF super featherweight title fight between Cassius Baloyi and Javier Osvaldo Alvarez in Kempton Park, South Africa. "It was a long flight to get there, but the people in South Africa were very friendly," she remembered. "I didn't have much time to sightsee, as I was there to do a job. Everything went well and I was invited back to South Africa to work another IBF fight less than two years later."

At the 2009 IBF International Convention in Panama City, Panama, Lee was selected to referee a fight for the IBF Latino light welterweight belt. National ring idols Roberto Duran and Eusebio Pedroza were in the crowd, along with top-flight IBF referees, judges and convention delegates. The fight between Heraclides Barrantes and Jose Hinestroza went off without a hitch, with Lee awarding it to the former on a sixth-round technical knockout. In a 2010 interview with Robert Mladinich of TheSweetScience.com, then–New York state commission chairman Ron Scott Stevens lauded Sparkle's ability. "She's really coming into her own and has a really good refereeing style," he said. "We've had women timekeepers, judges, and commissioners for many years, it was only natural that they would eventually want to expand into all areas of the game. They deserve to be where they are today because they are doing a great job."

For Lee, taking command of a fight starts in the boxers' locker rooms beforehand. "I tell them it is their job to prove to me that they can continue if they are hurt in the bout," she said. "To climb in the ring takes courage and I respect that, but I am there to protect the boxers and to enforce the rules. Sometimes I end up protecting a boxer from himself, as some would fight to the death if we didn't stop the fight.

"It's a humbling experience to be assigned to referee a fight, whether major or not," she added. "But it's not about the referee; it's about the participants, and I always try to do the best I can for them, and I pray that these warriors will go home safely to their families after the bout."

Just like when she wore a badge to work, Lee refuses to be intimidated when she steps into the ring for a fight—even when the contestants tower over her. "I have refereed some big heavyweights in my day," she said. "I remember one fight in which it seemed that the top of my head came up only to the waistband of one of the fighters as I went over the instructions in ring center. But I looked up and made sure he had no trouble understanding that when the bell rang he'd better do exactly as I ordered. And he did."

Lee retired from the police force in 2007, after twenty years on the job. Since then her out-of-the-ring time has been filled by her two grandchildren, church work, and serving as a volunteer youth counselor in Harlem.

14

John McCarthy

Referee "Big" John McCarthy may be the most recognizable official in combat sports today. As one of the faces of mixed-martial arts (MMA), he is the highest profile, most experienced, and one of the most respected MMA referees. McCarthy has worked the Ultimate Fighting Championship since its beginnings, and has also refereed the biggest MMA fights and appeared in television shows, movies, and video games. Readers may be surprised to see him in a book about boxing, but McCarthy also works as a boxing referee, having been involved with amateurs for years and recently moved into the professional ranks.

Like his father before him, McCarthy worked as a Los Angeles police officer, serving from 1985 until his retirement in 2007. Among his duties were patrol in South Central Los Angeles, Hollywood vice, narcotics, CRASH (an anti-gang special operations unit), and ultimately, the training academy. In 1992, riots occurred across Los Angeles following the acquittal of police officers who had been charged with using excessive force on Rodney King. One of the main defenses of the officers in the case was that they were following department policy. Subsequently, the Los Angeles Police Department began to review its use of force policies. Various martial artists from all disciplines were brought in to consult with police about new defensive tactics. McCarthy, who was assigned to the training academy teaching defensive tactics, was introduced to the Gracie family, practitioners of Brazilian Jiu-Jitsu.

The Gracie family was putting together a tournament featuring martial artists from various disciplines that would face off against each other in no-holds barred competition. That first tournament, dubbed The Ultimate Fighting Championship, was held on November 12, 1993, in Denver, Colorado. By this time, McCarthy was working closely and studying Jiu-Jitsu with the Gracies. He would go on to referee every Ultimate Fighting Championship event from UFC 2 to UFC 77, with the exception of UFC 70.

McCarthy was a natural fit for refereeing MMA. He was a practicing martial artist with a Brazilian Jiu-Jitsu black belt, is 6'4", 240 pounds, and, with his defensive tactics and police background, he was able to maintain control in the cage. Much as Mills Lane had done in boxing, McCarthy made the phrase, "Let's get it on!" his signature call to start the fight. He also worked as a commentator for the Fight Network and worked for Affliction Promotions. McCarthy played a role in drafting the unified rules of mixed martial arts and assisting in its regulation. "I do everything that a mixed martial artist does," he said. "I still spar, I wrestle, I roll [Brazilian Jiu-Jitsu]. Only I am not in competitions. I compete with myself, and it makes me better at refereeing."

Reflecting back on some of the epic battles he has worked, McCarthy said, "There are so many great fights, great martial artists that I have refereed, it is hard to pick my favorite fights and memories. I feel lucky to get to referee every fight I do. Doing the three fights between Randy Couture and Chuck Liddell was a great honor." Liddell and Couture, both former UFC champions, fought a trilogy of fights, with Liddell winning two of three. Those three UFC matches helped make mixed martial arts a mainstream sport and established the fighters as household names.

"It was an honor to referee Fedor [Emelianenko, an all-time heavyweight great] against Brett Rodgers, outside Chicago," he continued. "It was special to do the UFC heavyweight title fight between Junior dos Santos and Cain Velasquez. These are the things that make life what it is. You might not make a lot of money, but it is a great honor." Today, in addition to refereeing all over the world, McCarthy and his wife, Elaine, run Big John McCarthy's Ultimate Training Academy, a 28,500 square foot facility in Valencia, California. He conducts training seminars all over the country, which are certified by the Association of Boxing Commissions (ABC). He runs COMMAND (Certified Officials for Mixed Martial Arts National Development), a training course for referees and judges. In 2011, McCarthy released his autobiography, *Let's Get It On!: The Making of MMA and Its Ultimate Referee*, written with *Sports Illustrated* writer Loretta Hunt, which includes a great look at both McCarthy and MMA history. Like many people born before MMA was an organized sport, McCarthy started out as a boxing fan. "I grew up with boxing. My dad was a Los Angeles police officer. He would always go and take me to the Olympic Auditorium [a legendary Los Angeles fight arena]," he recalled. "I got to see Mando Ramos, Danny 'Little Red' Lopez, and Bobby Chacon. I loved boxing. I still love boxing. Great boxing is fantastic to watch. Great MMA is fantastic to watch. And bad boxing and bad MMA suck to watch. It is the whole competitive aspect, the great skill level."

There exists much debate between MMA and boxing fans as to who is "tougher," or who would win in a fight between a boxer and a mixed martial arts fighter. McCarthy, who has experience in both sports, can answer that question: "Each guy would win in his own discipline."

On August 28, 2010, there was a highly publicized mixed martial arts contest between former UFC light heavyweight and heavyweight champion Randy Couture, an MMA icon, and former middleweight, super middleweight, and cruiserweight boxing champion James Toney. Couture won by a very easy and early first round submission.

"Putting Toney in with Couture in a MMA fight was like swimming with the sharks and not knowing how to swim," McCarthy commented. "But it would have been the same thing if Toney faced Couture in a boxing ring. Couture would have been swimming with the sharks. "A boxer fighting MMA, everything they have been trained to do is counterproductive. The way they stand, their balance, the blading of their body," he explained. "If you try to change it, or say you are going to change it, once the lights go on for the fight, and the pressure is on, you are going to revert back to what you do. You return to what you are comfortable with."

Former Strikeforce welterweight champion and UFC star Nick Diaz is 1-0 as a professional boxer, having won a four-round decision in 2005. In 2011, he negotiated to fight faded former super middleweight champ Jeff Lacy in a boxing match. The fight never came off, with Diaz re-signing with the UFC. McCarthy feels that Lacy may have been too experienced in the boxing ring for Diaz to have defeated him but stated, "I think Nick would stand and bang with Lacy. Once he [Diaz] got hurt, I think he would realize what is best, and clinch Lacy."

McCarthy has been refereeing boxing for many years and has long been involved with the Police Games and Olympics in California. In 2009, he obtained his license to referee professional boxing in California. "I did it originally because there were a lot of hybrid shows, with both boxing and MMA." McCarthy has been active in the pro boxing ring since then, and highlights include refereeing a regional heavyweight title fight between Tye Fields and Nicolai Firtha.

McCarthy is one of the few top-notch referees who have done double duty with boxing and MMA and is in position to compare refereeing the two combat sports. "The difference between the sports is that what is legal in MMA is not legal in boxing. You have to put yourself in a different mindset for each sport," he explained. "In boxing, you have time to make decisions. In MMA, you can't take the time to make those decisions. In boxing, if someone goes down, the other fighter goes to a neutral corner. You take a look at the fallen fighter. If the fighter does not go to the neutral corner, you hold the count. You can send him to the neutral corner, and then resume the count."

McCarthy indicates that in a knockdown situation in MMA, you "make the decision [of whether to let the fight continue] on how the fighter goes down, did they put themselves in a position to defend themselves? What is the opponent doing? In MMA, you make the decisions much quicker; you don't have time on your side."

When asked to explain the incredible and rapid rise in popularity of MMA and perceived decline in popularity of boxing, McCarthy commented, "Both boxing and MMA are fantastic combat sports. Things seem to be going towards MMA.

"It is a generational thing, difference in generations," he continued, noting that the younger audience seems to be more drawn to MMA. "When I grew up, I rode motorcycles and skateboarded. And the things we thought were good then—they are nothing compared to the kids of today. Everything is bigger and better. It is like the X Games on ESPN. It is big with eighteen-year-old kids, who want to push things to the next level. MMA is the next level of fighting."

McCarthy did note that boxing, "the sweet science, it is an art. It is not just punching. Just like MMA, it is not all about the big pickup, sweeps, and kicks. It is an art."

McCarthy recognizes that boxing and MMA have different audiences. "You have to separate the two audiences," he said. "There is not a whole lot of crossover. It is limited. My dad, he is seventy-five years old. He was one of the biggest boxing fans. But bad promotions, bad decisions—now all he watches is MMA. However, McCarthy still sees a future for both sports. "If there are one hundred combat sports fans, forty five percent may be boxing fans, forty five percent may like MMA, and ten percent may like both."

15

Bruce McTavish

While on assignment in Thailand, Bruce McTavish left this message on a friend's cell phone: "Hi, just got out of prison in Bangkok." McTavish, however, had not been arrested. Rather, McTavish was talking about a boxing match he refereed earlier that day within the walls of Bangkok's Pathum Thani Correctional Institute for Women.

Few referees have experienced as many unique situations as Bruce McTavish over the last thirty years, both in and out of the ring. He has worked many high-profile international title bouts, including several involving Manny Pacquiao. McTavish has refereed fights in Siberia, North Korea, and China. He once had a gun held to his head by a cornerman upset because he thought McTavish acted hastily in stopping a bout.

McTavish, who was born in New Zealand, started boxing at the age of eight. After compiling an amateur record of 31-2, he hung up the gloves to get a degree in economics from Auckland University. He also played professional rugby in New Zealand and was a member of the country's national basketball team, which toured the Philippines in 1959.

McTavish returned to live in the Philippines in the early '70s when he accepted a position as national manager for Chrysler in the military sales division at Clark Air Base. He soon fell in love with and married Carmen

Tayag, daughter of noted author Renato Tayag. They settled in Angeles City, where he still lives.

Becoming a boxing referee was an easy transition. McTavish was training fighters in the Philippines before he started refereeing, and while a trainer he got to know the "Grand Old Man of Philippine Boxing"—Lope "Papa" Sarreal, whose twenty-two world champions included Sarreal's son-in-law, Gabriel "Flash" Elorde. Sarreal personally selected McTavish to referee an Oriental and Pacific Boxing Federation title fight in Manila in the early '70s.

"He was my mentor," said McTavish of Sarreal, "and he helped me a lot after a lot of blasphemy was given to me about my work in the ring. In those days it was hard; boxing was a tough sport in this country. You didn't get much credit; you got a lot of criticism. And Papa Sarreal always befriended me and helped me through the difficult times."

Boxing was one of the most popular sports in the Philippines during that time—much moreso than now, according to McTavish. "Without Manny Pacquiao, boxing would be just about forgotten today in the Philippines," he opined. "In those days it was very exciting. Very little money, but a lot of action. Angeles City was the mecca of boxing. A lot of fights were held in cockpit arenas, where two roosters fight each other to the death. There were a lot of sprained ankles on the canvas inside the cockpit, which had about a two-inch rise on it and had been sewn and repaired a million times."

What happened to McTavish one night at the Angeles City cockpit arena, however, was much scarier than a sprained ankle. He was refereeing an uneven fight in which one boxer was knocked down repeatedly early in the match, but he kept getting up until McTavish finally stopped it in the fourth round.

Then the beaten fighter's cornerman jumped into the ring to express his disagreement with McTavish's decision by pulling out a .45-caliber handgun and putting the barrel to his head.

"He said he was going to kill me because he lost a lot of money," recollected McTavish in an interview with Philippines-based boxing writer Ted Lerner in a June 15, 2009, interview. "He said that his fighter's strategy was to look bad in the early going so the other guy wore himself out, and then his guy would come back strong. I said, 'I wish you had told me that before the fight, and I wouldn't have stopped it. Next time I'll let him go,' and punctuated the lie with a conspiratorial wink I hoped would make him believe it. It worked. The man said, 'You are very lucky,' and put the gun away. I turned around so no one would see me wipe the beads of sweat off my forehead. I'll tell you, boxing teaches you diplomacy."

In another local fight, a boxer threw a haymaker—a wild and hard punch—that missed his opponent but connected with McTavish, fracturing several of his ribs. But McTavish hung in there, and ended up counting the iron-fisted fighter out in the match, with his opponent scoring a knockout victory. Afterward, McTavish told him, "You would have won the fight had you hit him with the punch that connected on me."

The Filipino capital of Manila was the site of one of the biggest fights in boxing history on October 1, 1975, when Muhammad Ali and Joe Frazier met for the third time in the so-called "Thrilla in Manila." Three American referees were under consideration to work the fight, but Frazier's trainer, Eddie Futch, didn't want any of them. Instead, native son Carlos Padilla, then a little-known referee, got the call. His handling of the action earned high praise, and soon afterwards Padilla moved to Las Vegas and became a high-profile referee, working championship fights involving Mike Tyson, Sugar Ray Leonard, and Julio Cesar Chavez, among others.

"Carlos was the first referee from the Philippines to gain international fame," stated McTavish. "He was also a mentor, and I am proud to call him my friend."

McTavish himself did not referee any bouts on the historic Ali vs. Frazier card, but he had a fight of his own sitting ringside with his wife, Carmen (whose dress ended up splashed with blood after Ali nailed Frazier with a right-cross and knocked out his mouthpiece). "I ended up whacking a guy who said that Frazier was 'a girl' for quitting," he said. "Joe didn't quit." The all-time classic ended with Ali winning by a fifteenth-round technical knockout when Hall of Fame trainer Futch refused to let Frazier come out for the final round.

After working his way up from the cockpit arena to become one of the islands' best referees, McTavish was sought after for important fights elsewhere. In 1985, he went to Australia for the bantamweight title match between champion Satoshi Shingaki from Japan and Jeff Fenech, who had captained the 1984 Aussie boxing team in the Olympic games and was trying to become the country's first world champion since Lionel Rose ruled the bantamweights in the late 1960s.

The fight at Hordern Pavilion in Sydney was only Fenech's seventh as a pro. It broke the attendance record at the Pavilion, which had been set eleven years earlier by crooner Frank Sinatra.

Shingaki took a one-sided beating in the fight, and McTavish stopped it in the ninth round even though the Japanese boxer hadn't gone down and protested the referee's action.

"[Shingaki's] brain was gone," McTavish said later. "Only his fitness was keeping him up. You could see it in his eyes," stated McTavish when interviewed in the 1988 book *Fenech: The Official Biography*. "A lot of people watching a fight think it's a fighter's legs that indicate when he's in trouble, but it's the eyes," he recalled. "I could see Satoshi's eyes start to go. He thought I was hitting him, and was looking at me. The crowd didn't see that. I stopped the bout without a knockdown and was criticized for it, but the audience couldn't see what I did.

"From experience you notice things and realize when a boxer is getting hurt. When Satoshi was looking at me and thinking I was hitting him, I knew he was in trouble and probably suffering from a concussion."

Being criticized for stopping a fight happens to all referees at some point in their careers, and it doesn't bother McTavish. "I never try to defend myself," he stated. "I think actions speak louder than words. I've made mistakes, but I try to limit them. I often review a fight that I have done to see what mistakes I might have made, so that I can try not to repeat them in the future."

On November 10, 2001, McTavish refereed a bout between Tirso Albia and Sayan Sanchat in Siberia's largest city, Novosibirsk. It was the first international title fight in that section of the former Soviet Union. That was one mistake he didn't repeat.

"It took almost forty hours to get there, and the weather in Siberia was absolutely bone-chilling," he recalled. "Outdoors it was way sub-zero and

Bernard Hopkins and Kelly Pavlik mix it up. In their October 2008 contest, the ageless wonder Hopkins again turned back the clock and won a decision over the undefeated middleweight champion Pavlik. Referee Benjy Esteves is the third man in the ring. *Courtesy of photographer Ray Bailey*

"Big" John McCarthy gives pre-fight instructions to MMA heavyweight contender Fabricio Werdum prior to his historic upset submission win over Fedor Emelianenko in June 2010, ending Emelianenko's twenty-eight-fight winning streak. Fellow MMA contender Renato "Babalu" Sobral is pictured in the bottom right corner. *Courtesy of John McCarthy*

Denny Nelson directs Hall of Famer Ken Norton to a neutral corner after Norton knocked down former conqueror Jose Luis Garcia in their August 14, 1975, bout. *Courtesy of photographer Tom Casino*

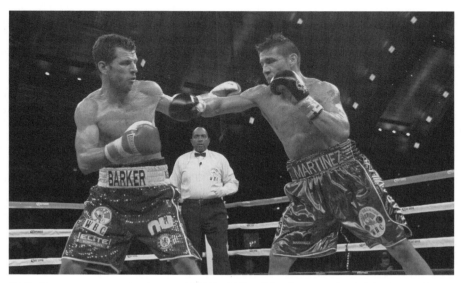

Eddie Cotton oversees action between WBC middleweight champion Sergio Martinez and challenger Darren Barker in their October 1, 2011, bout in Atlantic City, New Jersey. *Courtesy of photographer Ray Bailey*

ABOVE: The great Frank Cappuccino doing what he was known for—letting the fighters fight. *Courtesy of photographer Ray Bailey*

RIGHT: Frank Garza enjoys a break in the action. *Courtesy of photographer Drayonah Abramski*

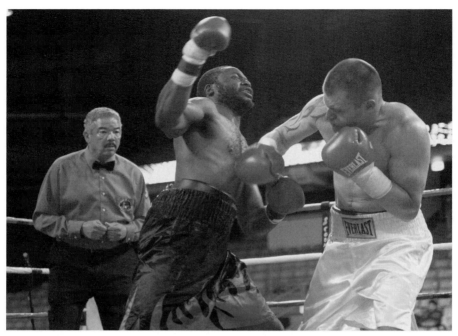

"Gentleman" Gerald Scott watches in on the action intently. *Courtesy of photographer Tom Barnes*

Kenny Bayless (left), with twin brother Kermit, an established California-based boxing judge (right), and the late legendary former heavyweight champion Smokin' Joe Frazier. *Courtesy of photographer Mary Ann Owen*

Muhammad Ali gets directed to a neutral corner by Mills Lane after knocking down light heavyweight champion Bob Foster in their November 1972 match up. All three were participants in the 1960 Olympic Boxing Trials as boxers. Ali, then eighteen years old and fighting under his birth name, Cassius Clay, won a gold medal in the 1960 Olympics at light heavyweight. *Courtesy of Tommy Lane*

Mike Tyson became the youngest fighter to win the heavyweight title on November 22, 1986, at the age of twenty, against Trevor Berbick, in this bout refereed by Mills Lane. Tyson destroyed Berbick inside of two rounds. *Courtesy of Tommy Lane*

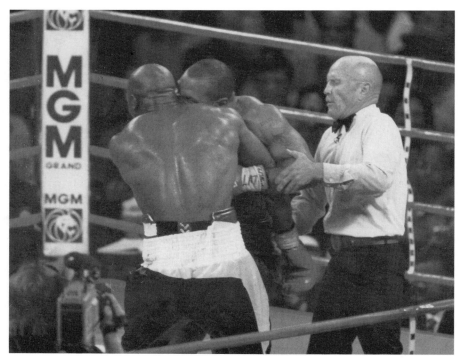

Hall of Fame referee Mills Lane steps in as Mike Tyson bites the ear of Evander Holyfield. Tyson would be disqualified in the third round of the June 28, 1997, bout. At the time, the fight broke all pay-per-view, foreign sales, closed circuit, and live gate records, as the highest grossing boxing match in history. *Courtesy of Tommy Lane*

Jack Reiss raises the hand of the victor, Tim Bradley, after a 2010 bout. *Courtesy of photographer Big Joe Miranda*

Pat Russell was the referee for the third meeting between Rafael Marquez and Israel Vazquez in their 2008 war, which Vazquez won. The two warriors fought four times, each winning twice. Russell was also a judge in the boxers' first meeting, won by Marquez, the brother of fellow Mexican great, Juan Manuel Marquez. *Courtesy of photographer Paul Gallegos*

Pete Podgorski with North American Boxing Federation (NABF) champ John Brown, and trainer and former world light heavyweight champion Eddie Mustafa Muhammad. *Courtesy of Pete Podgorski*

Rafael Ramos is the third man for the WBO 122-pound title fight between Nonito Donaire and Wilfredo Vazquez Jr. This marked the fourth division that Donaire had won a title in. *Courtesy of photographer Sumio Yamada*

English referee Mickey Vann speaks to Amir Khan (left); Mickey Vann in his fighting days (right). *Courtesy of Mickey Vann*

Retired great Richard Steele is still going strong and giving back to the community through boxing. Steele has refereed many of the greatest matches in boxing history. *Courtesy of photographer Mary Ann Owen*

World class referee Vic Drakulich of Reno has also enjoyed great success outside of the ring as a civil litigator. *Courtesy of photographer Mary Ann Owen*

The always professional John O'Brien oversees action at the UIC Pavilion in Chicago between Joshua Rodriguez and Jaime Herrera. O'Brien is the longtime chief official of the Chicago Golden Gloves, one of the United States' most prestigious amateur tournaments. *Courtesy of photographer Tom Barnes*

Rising referee Celestino Ruiz in his young boxing days (center, front row). Ruiz's former coach Mauro DiFiore (back row, second from the left) is now a highly regarded boxing judge. Then lightweight contender, Johnny Lira (third from the left), and then heavyweight contender, James "Quick" Tillis (far right), are also pictured. *Courtesy of Celestino Ruiz*

Sparkle Lee stands out as a top referee and is a female in a male-dominated occupation. *Courtesy of photographer VPeiPics*

Referee Rudy Battle post-fight with the winner, and all-time great, Bernard Hopkins. *Courtesy of photographer Ray Bailey*

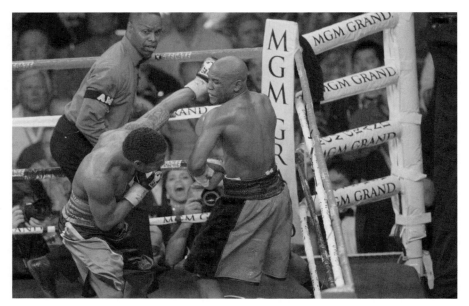

Three of the best in the business, referee Kenny Bayless, "Sugar" Shane Mosley, and Floyd Mayweather Jr. In recent years, perhaps no one has refereed as many high-profile bouts as Bayless. *Courtesy of photographer Mary Ann Owen*

Tony Weeks looks on as Ricky "Hitman" Hatton beats Juan Urango. *Courtesy of photographer Mary Ann Owen*

Up-and-coming boxing referee Celestino Ruiz with Hall of Fame referee Joe Cortez. *Courtesy of Celestino Ruiz*

World Boxing Organization (WBO) super middleweight champion Joe Calzaghe gets his hand raised by referee Mark Nelson. *Courtesy of photographer Alan Whiter, Action Images*

The great Wayne Kelly raises the hand of victorious Raymond Serrano. Kelly, one of boxing's best referees, a social worker, and Vietnam veteran, passed away shortly after being interviewed for this book. *Courtesy of photographer VPeiPics*

Robert Byrd has distinguished himself both inside and outside the ring as one of boxing's finest referees, a Marine Corps veteran, and a police commander. *Courtesy of Robert Byrd*

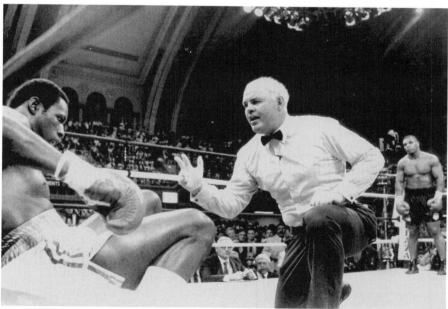

Former heavyweight contender turned referee Randy Neumann administers the count to Carl "The Truth" Williams in his bout versus Mike Tyson on July 21, 1989. Tyson won by technical knockout in ninety-three seconds to retain his unified heavyweight title at the Convention Center in Atlantic City, New Jersey. *Courtesy of Randy Neumann*

Veteran referee Steve Smoger has long been considered an elite third man. Here he begins to administer a count over a downed fighter. *Courtesy of Steve Smoger*

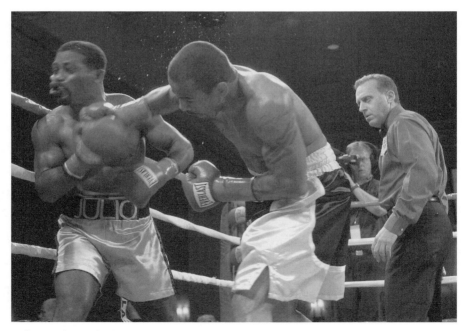

Referee Jack Reiss looks on as Verno Phillips, who held the IBF, WBU (World Boxing Union), and WBO junior middleweight titles, lands a crushing knockout blow on Julio Garcia in their 2004 IBF title elimination fight. *Courtesy of photographer Paul Gallegos*

the fight was held, of all places, in a hockey rink called the Ice Palace. The ice under the floorboards made the place so cold I got very sick.

"After the fight I was invited back to referee another one," he said, "but I told them that I didn't want to hog all the plum assignments and they should give the opportunity to someone else. It was the most gracious way I could think of to get out of it."

Even more forbidding than Siberia was North Korea, the closed-up, belligerently Communist enclave with a perpetual us-against-the-world complex. When McTavish was assigned to referee there in 2007, he joked, "I wondered what I had done wrong."

The occasion was the World Boxing Council female super flyweight championship fight between native Myung Ok Ryu and Ana Maria Torres, a joint promotion effort between the South Korean Professional Boxing Commission and the boxing hierarchy in North Korea. It was the first pro boxing event staged in Gaeseong City—the historical former Korean capital located about one hour's drive from Seoul and the only major city to change hands as a result of the Korean War.

North Koreans share the same language and some common culture with the South Koreans, but materially they live very different lives from those south of the 38th parallel. Rigidly isolationist, North Korea does not gladly welcome outsiders. All foreign visitors are closely monitored and must be constantly on their guard and watch what they say and how they act, because the government is unstintingly alert for signs of what the authorities consider insulting—and therefore illegal—behavior.

After arriving in Seoul, McTavish boarded a bus for North Korea. On it were representatives of the South Korean Boxing Commission, the boxing judges assigned to the fight, and participating boxers and trainers that were not from North Korea.

Upon passing into North Korea, their suitcases were searched for contraband and military officials appropriated all cameras and passports. The visitors were housed in a traditional Korean hotel room where guests slept on mats on a heated floor and hot water was available only a few hours a day. The hotel's main entrance was guarded by military personnel to keep the guests from going on any unauthorized excursions. Every foreign boxing official was assigned his own personal North Korean "guide" whose job was to watch his every move.

The evening before the title fight, the official weigh-in ceremony was held in a small banquet facility on the grounds of the hotel. Afterward, a traditional Korean meal was served along with some North Korean wine and spirits. Mike Fitzgerald (who lives in Janesville, Wisconsin, and is coauthor of this book), was one of the judges assigned to the fight and the only one involved in the event besides McTavish whose native language was English. "At dinner, each foreign boxing official was seated next to his North Korean guide," Fitzgerald recalled. "The guides were all young men dressed in dark suits. They wore impassive expressions, had a good command of English, and followed us everywhere we went.

"Bruce has a great sense of humor, and during the dinner he made a point of proposing numerous toasts to his guide's health, happiness, family, the brotherhood of nations, and anything else he could think of. The guides were supposed to always be polite, so every time Bruce made a toast his guide did the same. By the end of the night Bruce's formerly restrained and impassive guide was hugging everybody in sight. It was hilarious."

Before the fight the next day all the officials attended a rules meeting. "I think Bruce and I were the only two people in North Korea who did not smoke," said Fitzgerald. "There were ten chairs and fifteen ashtrays in the meeting room. Bruce and I were the first people in there, and he hid all the ashtrays before the other officials arrived. I had a difficult time keeping a straight face as all the North and South Korean boxing officials searched frantically for somewhere to dump their ashes."

The fight was held in a small basketball gymnasium packed with partisan fans. Attendance was by government invitation only. There were no fight posters or tickets printed.

In a close duel, Myung Ok Ryu won the decision and the title.

Immediately afterward, the boxing officials boarded a bus and departed for Seoul. It was just before sunset, and there were few cars on the road and an occasional bicycle rider. In the fields farmers worked using ox-pulled plows.

"It was sad and frightening," said McTavish. "People in North Korea are literally dying of malnutrition thanks to their government's tyranny. But they put on a show to impress us, even to the point of having people wearing expensive designer outfits walking around the streets near our hotel. They were always the same people wearing the same outfits, acting out a charade for our benefit."

On April 3, 2007, McTavish refereed at the Klong Prem Central Prison for Women in Bangkok, where Thailand's Samson Tor Buamas fought Ayaka Miyao for the vacant WBC women's light flyweight title. That's where Samson, whose real name is Siriporn Thaweesuk, was serving a ten-year sentence on drug charges since being convicted in 2000 at the age of seventeen. Thai inmates are encouraged to participate in sports, and imprisoned boxers who win a world title are granted their freedom for bringing honor to their country.

The bout was staged in an open-air arena on the grounds of the prison. Only a few specially chosen inmates were allowed to view the action in person. The rest watched on television. Samson became an instant national hero by defeating Miyao by unanimous decision. Her photo graced the front page of every newspaper in the country the next day, and she went into the record books as the first prison inmate to win a world boxing title. She was officially pardoned by the king and released from prison with three years remaining on her sentence.

"I will never forget it," said McTavish. "The prison fight was historical and educational. The average person from the so-called modern world would find it very difficult to survive in such an environment. The tension during the fight was electrifying. But I was treated very well at the prison. I received a drink and a sandwich from an Australian I first thought was an exchange warden, but who turned out to be an inmate trustee."

Ted Lerner is a boxing announcer in the Philippines and is the country's boxing correspondent for *The Ring* magazine. "I've worked with Bruce on countless fights as an announcer and watched a hundred more where he was the referee," he said. "I've always liked his style in the ring. He stays out of the fighters' way and doesn't impose himself on the fight unnecessarily just to get his face on the TV."

McTavish always goes over the rules with the boxers in their locker rooms before a fight. "So he has already established firm control before they even get in the ring," indicated Lerner. "He never gives instructions in the ring because he knows the fighters aren't paying attention then. He also makes great decisions in the ring. He lets the fighters work their way out of a clinch. I know for a fact he has the safety of the fighters as his first and highest priority, and won't hesitate to stop a fight, even with just seconds remaining, to protect a fighter from serious harm. Bruce is one of the finest referees in the world, and any fight he refs will certainly be fair." McTavish loves what he does but confesses that the long-distance traveling required of a top referee has gotten old. "Now it's a bit of a pain," he admits, "and if I could just press a button and be at the fight, that would be fine with me. But I still love everything else about the job."

He stays in shape for the physical rigors of refereeing by performing forty-five minutes of calisthenics every day and jogging five days a week.

McTavish doesn't keep his boxing savvy to himself. "When a young referee comes up and asks me to critique them, I don't hold back," he said. "I admire them and I go out of my way to help as much as I can. I stress things like proper positioning, where to stand, when to move, and when not to move. I have seen two or three in the Philippines that have come on very well just because they have gone out of their way to improve themselves."

He also advises newbies to go easy on the grub on the day of an assignment. "I see so many referees that have a full meal twenty minutes before they get into the ring, and their movements are tired and logy. I'll eat some pasta or a salad early the day of the fight, and that's it."

The current and probably all-time greatest idol in Filipino boxing is Manny Pacquiao. In 2009, news reports said he was the sixth highest paid athlete in the world, having earned more than $40 million that year. McTavish has known the superstar since Pacquiao was just another urchin with dreams of boxing glory.

"Manny spent some time in my hometown of Angeles City when he was in his teens, and I got to known him then," he remembered. "Rick Staheli, an American living here, trained him at the time, and Manny became like a son to me. I negotiated his first title fight against Chatchai

Sasakul. He was a respectful kid and we trained him hard and he never complained and was a good listener. I'm proud to have watched him grow into a mature adult and a good family man."

McTavish refereed several of Pacquiao's bouts in the Philippines and still maintains a close friendship with the boxing icon.

"Take a guy like Muhammad Ali," he stated in an interview with Ted Lerner. "You could never get anyone to learn how to box by watching Muhammad Ali. There's only one Ali. Then you get a Prince [Naseem] Hamed. You definitely wouldn't want to teach someone to fight that way, either.

"Then along comes a Manny Pacquiao, a diamond in the rough and maybe the greatest diamond in the world. You got the Alis, the Hameds, and then you've got the Manny Pacquiaos. It's something special. You can't train them to be like that. They're just freaks of nature." Outside the ring, one of McTavish's passions is community involvement. An active Rotarian for thirty years, he has served as president of his local Rotary chapter and has spearheaded the effort to raise funds to see to the needs of more than forty young orphans. He is also active in the campaign to provide polio vaccinations for thousands of impoverished children.

In 2003, when former Philippine bantamweight champion Alvin Felicilda required two brain surgeries after being knocked out in a fight in Japan, McTavish and others in the boxing community got together to raise money for medical and rehabilitation expenses. McTavish personally delivered the donations to Felisilda's hometown.

Now in his late sixties, McTavish admits that the thought of retirement occasionally crosses his mind. He is currently the WBC's ring officials' secretary and has been directing the organization's referees' seminars for a decade or so. But he's not ready to put away his bowtie for good, yet.

"Recently as I was waiting in the ring for the boxers to come in for a fight, I felt that familiar tingle in my spine," said McTavish. "The rush was there—the lights, the crowd, the ambiance. When I lose that, then I'll know it's time to hang it up.

"I know guys who are thirty-five or forty who shouldn't be refereeing. It depends on your diet and your overall fitness and ability to move. When my legs start to go, I'll go."

16

Denny Nelson

Minnesota referee Denny Nelson often flew to Las Vegas with his wife, Marlys, to watch boxers train for mega-fights at Caesars Palace. On one of these trips in 1984, he bumped into famous retired referee Jay Edson, who'd worked bouts featuring such fistic gods as Sugar Ray Leonard, George Foreman, and Muhammad Ali before becoming a coordinator for promoter Bob Arum's "Top Rank" organization.

Nelson had been a boxing referee for more than twelve years then but hadn't worked much outside the Gopher State. He wanted to change that. "No referee from Minnesota had ever worked a fight out of the country, and I thought I was more than ready for that giant step," he remembered.

Edson recommended that Nelson contact the International Boxing Federation, which was looking to add experienced referees to its roster. Barely a year later, Nelson worked an IBF fight in Daejeon, South Korea—the first of many international refereeing assignments for the man whose career in boxing started many years earlier when he tagged along to the gym with his older brother, Marty.

"From then on I was just hooked on boxing and started competing as an amateur," Nelson recalled of his childhood. "I never was involved in street fights as a kid, and in amateur boxing my goal was to always out-think my opponent."

He out-thought enough of them to advance to the National Golden Gloves Tournament of Champions at Chicago Stadium three times in the 1950s. Eventually he turned pro and was undefeated in a handful of fights, but after marrying and starting a family, he hung up the gloves.

"I knew how good I was," he stated, "which probably wasn't good enough to be a world champion. But boxing was in my blood, and I remained close to the sport as a trainer and director of the Minnesota Golden Gloves program for years.

"Initially, officiating didn't excite me," Nelson recalled. "I had seen plenty of officials booed and harassed at boxing shows and I had seen some referees actually argue with people in the crowd during a bout. None of that appealed to me."

That changed in the early 1970s, when Nelson decided to apply for a professional referee's license with the Minnesota boxing commission. After an apprenticeship in the preliminary ranks, he worked his way up to main events and eventually became St. Paul's resident referee.

By then big-time boxing had returned to the area as home state heavy-weight Scott LeDoux began fighting his way up the ranks. It wasn't an easy process. "The Fighting Frenchman" was undefeated when he met journey-man Roy Wallace in St. Paul in 1975. Nelson was the third man in the ring that night, and when LeDoux incurred a bad cut in the second round Nelson stopped the fight in favor of Wallace.

"Scott wanted to continue fighting, and let me know how he felt about my call in no uncertain terms," recollected Nelson. "Eventually we got back on good terms. Sometimes a referee needs to protect a boxer like LeDoux from himself because he has so much courage."

Top heavyweight contender Ken Norton was coming off a sensational knockout victory over Jerry Quarry and was matched in St. Paul with Jose Luis Garcia, who'd knocked Norton out a few years earlier. The August 14, 1975, bout aired on *The CBS Sports Spectacular*, with Pat Summerall host-ing the broadcast, and commentary by Angelo Dundee, Muhammad Ali's trainer.

"I have no idea how this fight ever landed in St. Paul," said Nelson, "but I was happy to get the refereeing assignment from the commission the day before. As is customary, I met with both fighters in their locker rooms before the fight to go over the rules. Norton was a tremendous body puncher, and I warned him a few times during our pre-fight meeting to keep his punches up during the bout."

Norton ended the rough fight in the fifth round with a body shot. "When Norton ran into me at the post-fight celebration, he smiled widely and said, 'Keep your punches up!'" recalled Nelson.

The ring is usually no place for laughter, but Nelson had to fight to keep a straight face one night when an overmatched fighter he was count-ing over opened his eyes and said, "I'm out!" and then closed them again until Nelson had tolled off the full ten-count.

But Nelson didn't take any nonsense from well-known loser Bruce "The Mouse" Strauss when he refereed Strauss's fight with Billy Goodwin in the small town of Amery, in northwestern Wisconsin. Strauss publicly bragged about having been knocked out on every continent except Antarctica. After he retired, a movie called *Mouse* came out about his questionable boxing exploits. Before the Goodwin fight, Wisconsin commissioner Vern Woodward told Strauss that he had better fight on the level that night. Well-known Madison trainer Bob Lynch was in the house, and remembers with delight that the Mouse not only went the full ten rounds, but actually won the decision. "It was thanks, too, to referee Denny Nelson," Lynch recalled in an interview with the authors. "He did an excellent job, and Strauss gave him no bullshit."

"The main responsibility of any referee is the safety of the boxers," stated Nelson. "My next concerns are to keep the fight clean and for me to stay out of the way of the action. A referee needs to understand the rules and know how to implement them. Through my years as a referee the philoso-phy of the position changed, with more of an emphasis placed on the safety of the participants. I've always tried not to make decisions too quickly in the ring. You can't jump to conclusions in the heat of battle. It's important to take your time and make the right call for the boxers involved. One bad call could change the career of a fighter.

"Sometimes it is just a matter of common sense and just being fair," he continued. "I always tell the boxers in the dressing room before the fight that I don't want to have to take any points from them during the fight. I want the winner to be victorious based on his own ability."

In a 1984 clash for the Minnesota state light middleweight title between Brian Brunette and Gary Holmgren, Nelson simultaneously served as referee and a judge, as was customary in the state at that time. Brunette won the close bout on a majority-decision. Afterwards Nelson went to the commission to recommend that from then on three ringside judges be used to score a fight so the referee could concentrate on his duties inside the ropes.

"The commission was concerned about the increased expense to the promoter of adding another official," recalled Nelson. "But Minnesota was starting to get some big fights with ranked contenders, and I felt it was too much on a referee to score the same bout he was refereeing. Most other state commissions were using three judges to score a fight at that time. I argued that maintaining the boxers' safety and making sure the rules were properly enforced was enough responsibility for a referee."

The commission listened to its resident expert, and Minnesota went with three judges.

When Nelson finally got his first international assignment from the IBF—the January 25, 1985, Jong-Kwan Chung vs. Soon-Chun Kwon IBF flyweight championship fight in South Korea—he was forty-seven years old. The first thing he did was call home and tell his wife to start packing.

"As I learned later on, it isn't normal protocol to bring one's wife along on a boxing assignment," he said. "But I wanted Marlys to be part of what I thought could be a once-in-a-lifetime experience. I'm glad she went, too, as the Korean boxing commissioner spoke a bit of English but all the other officials and the boxers were Korean, and my wife was the only one with whom I had a conversation of any length the whole time we were there.

"I remember getting picked up at the airport and being driven to Daejeon," he continued. "It was cold outside but there were Korean women washing clothes in the river. The language, food and culture were so different than back home. But it was a great experience for us."

The fight itself turned out to be a war. "After the fourteenth round, I called in the doctor to assess the fighters' condition because they had both taken major punishment," said Nelson. "Right after he said it was OK for them to continue, the boxing commissioner jumped up and in broken English said, 'Mr. Nelson, you will let this contest continue!' But it was the physician's opinion I relied on. I would have stopped the contest if I felt it was the right call.

"When the final bell rang, I had no idea who had won the fight. The judges' scores were the announced in Korean, of course, which I didn't understand. They first raised defending champion Soon-Chun Kwon's hand, and I assumed he had won. But then they announced Jong-Kwan Chung's name and raised his hand. I was confused and didn't know who won the fight until my cab driver explained on the ride back to the hotel that it was a draw. Kwon's hand was raised first because he was the champion."

Nelson's next international assignment was to referee the IBF super fly-weight title fight in Jakarta, Indonesia, between Ellyas Pical and Cesar Polanco. He was glad Marlys didn't accompany him this time when he and the other imported officials were warned about bandits targeting foreigners in the area. Each official was assigned his own personal security guard for the duration of his stay. "That gave me some comfort," he stated, "until I met my security person. He was smaller than me and I'm not a big guy."

As he made his way to the ring for the fight, Nelson noticed armed security guards posted throughout the facility. "There was a lot of poverty in Jakarta," he recalled, "and there were many people outside the arena who couldn't afford a ticket and were trying to sneak in. It was a little startling to see."

But it was the intense heat and humidity bothered him the most. "The fight went the full fifteen rounds," Nelson remembered. "I always prided myself on staying in shape, but at the end I was tired. From that point on I took up jogging to increase my fitness level."

One of Nelson's favorite memories was refereeing the IBF light middleweight title fight between Canadian hero Matthew Hilton and Buster Drayton on June 27, 1987. The venue was the historic Montreal Forum, where the 1976 Olympic boxing finals, and several Stanley Cup hockey championship games, were held. Before a packed house, Hilton won a close but unanimous fifteen-round decision.

Sometimes, just getting to a foreign locale is a battle in itself. Once when Nelson was scheduled to work a fight in Argentina, he was stranded for more than ten hours at the Atlanta airport because of a huge cloud of volcanic ash over Argentina. It's dangerous for airplanes to fly in and near volcanic ash because it might gum up the engines and put the plane in jeopardy. When the cloud dissipated enough for flights to Argentina to resume, Nelson made it there just in time for the fight. "I was tired from the hassle, but there was nothing I could do about it," he said. "You just have to push it out of your mind and get the job done."

After Nelson refereed a bout in Acapulco, Mexico, in 1990, the promoter announced to the officials that since he had not made it to the bank, everyone would be paid in Mexican currency. "I ended up with $1,800 in pesos stuffed in my pants pockets and my suitcase," Nelson recalled. "It gave me some concern about what might happen at the airport or customs, but there was no problem."

When he was in Cape Town, South Africa, to work a fight, Nelson and the bout's other officials were taken on a tour of a nearby township where the poverty was so widespread that the local boxing gym had a dirt floor. When the group returned to the hotel headquarters, they found that burglars had broken into the safe and stolen everyone's wallet and passport. "It was difficult getting back to the States," Nelson remembered. "We had to get a letter from the U.S. Consulate explaining what had happened, and it still took a while at the airport in New York City to get everything sorted out."

When Nelson is sent on an overseas assignment, he's all business, unlike one of the judges assigned to a fight Denny refereed in Bangkok. "I came down for breakfast in the hotel," he recalled, "and saw this fellow just coming in from a night out on the town. He was still drunk. He thought he was on vacation, I guess. He didn't judge the fight that night, and I haven't seen or heard anything about him since.

"The deal is, it's a privilege to be asked to referee or judge a world title fight," said Nelson. "I represent the organization that assigned me, and my only objective is to get the job done correctly. It's not a party. I usually spend the afternoon of a fight relaxing in my hotel room. If I am at a unique location for an annual officials' convention, I will take in some tourist destinations; but when I'm refereeing or judging a fight you will usually find me at the hotel, either in my room or mingling with the other officials working the contest."

Often a referee will be the target of attempted intimidation by a boxer's handlers. This happened to Nelson, who was third man when Michael Nunn risked his world middleweight title against undefeated James Toney in the champion's hometown of Davenport, Iowa, on May 10, 1991. Nunn's chief second for the fight was legendary trainer Angelo Dundee. "Dundee came up to me in the ring before the fight and started complaining about all the people over in Toney's corner," stated Nelson. "He ordered me to go over and tell them that some of the people had to leave. This was funny because over in Nunn's corner there were even more people than in Toney's. I just blew it off. There's only one guy in each corner who does the fighting. Handlers will try for any advantage, and you can't let it affect you."

Nunn was leading going into the eleventh round, but then a Toney left hook found its mark and down went the champion. "He beat the count and told me he was all right," recalled Nelson, "so I let it continue. But then he was knocked down again and I stopped the fight."

Over the next several years Nelson worked title fights in Italy, Germany, Denmark, and England, as well as in his home base of St. Paul and elsewhere around the United States. He shared the ring with such champions as Felix Trinidad, Joey Gamache, Orlando Canizales, Virgil Hill, and Johnny Tapia.

In 2006 he decided to hang up his bowtie. "It was just time," said Nelson. "I wanted to go out when I still felt I could get the job done. I didn't want to stay on too long."

He still works as a boxing judge at home and abroad and very proudly follows the career of his son, Mark, who has followed in his footsteps as a successful and in-demand international referee.

"Mark's achievements have already way exceeded mine," said Nelson with obvious satisfaction. "I refereed my first international world title fight at age forty-seven. Mark is in his mid-forties, and he has already done about sixty world title fights!"

17

Mark Nelson

When he conducts seminars on the art and science of refereeing professional boxing matches, Mark Nelson draws laughs by saying, "Nobody pays to see the referee in the ring, except maybe his mother."

Nelson spent years learning what a referee does before he ever climbed into the ring to do it himself. As a youth he tagged along to seminars, fight cards, and boxing gyms with his father, respected international referee Denny Nelson. "I went to everything possible with my dad and tried to absorb as much as I could at seminars and by asking him questions," said Mark. "He never pushed me to be a referee, it was my idea. I got in the ring once as an amateur boxer. I always joke that I lost a controversial split-decision at age fifteen, and then retired. But my goal was to be a referee."

A professional referee since 1992, Nelson has traveled the globe refereeing fights of international import; but he is just as thrilled to work club shows in his native Minnesota and around the Midwest. "I've always felt that whether it's a four-round preliminary fight or one for the championship of the world, that fight is the most important fight in the world to the two fighters in the ring," he stated. "If you don't take the same approach regardless of the magnitude of the fight, you are doing the sport and its participants a disservice."

Whether in North Dakota or Berlin, Germany, his pre-fight ritual doesn't vary. "I form a relationship with the other officials working the fight with me," said Nelson. "I make sure to meet with the timekeeper and discuss the importance of hitting the bell loud enough. And I tell him to keep hitting it until he's certain I've heard it. There have been times when a round ends and only one of the fighters heard the bell, and the action continued and someone got knocked out, resulting in controversy, a no-contest, or disqualification.

"I also make sure to also meet with the doctor and judges. I may need to rely on the judges for their viewpoint in the case of a cut fighter. I may ask if the cut was caused by a punch or a head-butt. It's important to make the right call. Referees, including myself, do make mistakes. Careers hinge on our decisions, so we'd better do everything possible to get it right."

Beginning in 1989, Mark worked as an amateur referee in Minnesota and continued to attend professional boxing seminars with his father. At one of them he videotaped the presentation by storied referee Mills Lane, one of Nelson's favorites. "I still watch the video," he said. "I also have videos of fights that Mills refereed and I watch them periodically and pick up tips. Mills was actually shorter than me in stature, but he was absolutely in charge in the ring."

In 1992 there were six licensed professional boxing officials in Minnesota trained to referee and judge fights. When one of them retired, Nelson was reluctant to leave the amateurs, but when no one else applied for the vacancy, he went for it. "I put together a résumé and went before the board that oversees boxing in Minnesota," he said. "Scott LeDoux, the former heavyweight contender, was the chairman. He spoke up, paid me some compliments, and made a motion to accept my application for a professional license. It was approved, and to my surprise, Executive Director Jim O'Hara then told me I would be working a professional show the following week."

While he admired Mills Lane, Nelson's primary role model and mentor is closer to home. "My dad has helped me so much," he stated. "He was always generous and helpful when critiquing my work in those early days. Like most dads, he tried to steer clear of negativity. But when we'd watch fights on TV, he would point out something the referee was doing and say, 'Don't do that,' if it was an unwarranted intrusion in the fight, or he'd praise the referee for handling a situation in the right way."

The homeschooling paid off. After just two years, Mark was off to Italy to work a twelve-round contest for the IBF Intercontinental title between local hero Michele Piccirillo and Viktor Baranov. He ended up doing double duty that night, both referring and judging the fight after one of the Italian judges withdrew following a conflict with the local commission. It was no problem for Nelson (except when it came to marking his scorecard between rounds, which was difficult on account of his latex gloves), and he even got paid extra.

World title fight assignments soon followed, taking Nelson to Hungary and England. So did some hard lessons in endurance and world geography. When the World Boxing Union called on him to referee in Thailand on April 18, 1997, Mark recalled, "I didn't recognize the name of the city where the fight would be held, but my final flight destination was Bangkok. It was the longest commute I ever made. My initial flight left from Minneapolis at 6 a.m., with a transfer in Phoenix, followed by a twelve-hour layover in Los Angeles. Then I boarded a plane for a fourteen-hour flight to Taipai, and after a six-hour layover there I was finally off to Bangkok.

"In Bangkok, I sat through a two-hour traffic jam on the way to my hotel. When I got there my supervisor said, 'Go upstairs and take your time, dinner is not for another twenty minutes!' Then he told me that we needed to catch an early flight the next day to the northeastern Thai province of Udon Thani. I had thought the fight was somewhere on the outskirts of Bangkok. I was gone about five days, total, and was on ten different airplanes. But it was all worth it."

To prevent misunderstandings in the ring, Nelson goes over the rules with the boxers in their locker rooms before a fight. "I tell them what I expect from them and their handlers, and make sure they understand that the chief second is the only person I will talk to in the corner during the fight," he stated.

"I also tell the boxers that it is an honor to referee their bout and that I have the utmost respect for what they do—and that I expect the same from them. I tell them that I don't like to take points away, but will do so if necessary to enforce the rules."

Nelson emphasizes that his number one job is to watch out for the fighters' personal safety, his ultimate goal being that they return safely to their families and friends after the fight.

Once a boxer in a preliminary bout on a card in Minnesota took umbrage at that. "I'll die in that ring!" he told Nelson with exaggerated bravado. "I have no family. I have nothing, and am willing to die!"

Nelson didn't mince word, telling the foolhardy fighter, "You won't be dying in my ring tonight or any other time I referee one of your fights!"

In August 1998, Nelson went to a small city in Sicily called Calatafimi to referee a World Boxing Union middleweight title fight between champion Silvio Branco and Guyana's Anthony Andrews.

"The day before the bout," Nelson recalled, "they said they were going take me and the other officials to meet 'The Guy.' I had no idea who this was, but it sounded kind of ominous. It turned out that 'The Guy' was a top Sicilian political figure who worked in a place bigger than the White House. At the entrance we had to surrender our passports and then go through several locked doors to get to his office. He didn't speak English, so conversation was stilted. He gave me a book on the history of Sicily written in English and some cigars. 'The Guy' was just a fight fan, and a pretty nice guy."

On a 1999 assignment in Oregon to referee Diego Corrales's IBF super featherweight title defense against John Brown, Nelson refereed a co–main event with Joe Cortez, the well-known Nevada-based referee who worked the night's other televised event between Fernando Vargas and Ronald "Winky" Wright. After the fights, Nelson and Cortez went out to dinner to compare notes about their craft and the state of boxing in general.

"Joe said it was a shame I lived in a state that wasn't a hotbed of ring action," recalled Nelson. "I have sent inquiries to Las Vegas about working there, but it would mean a permanent move. Right now I'm happy with my life in Minnesota. I'm happy to work as much as possible on my home turf, and the overseas assignments I get are always great and, I think, a testament to my ability."

Cortez has become another mentor for Nelson. "Before a lot of my title fights, I call him up and we run through different possible scenarios," he said. "When I'm in Vegas I'll go over to Joe's house and we'll get in his boxing ring and work on things. I'm always running various scenarios through my head to be as prepared as possible for what could happen in that ring."

While attending the World Boxing Association's 2003 convention in Indonesia, Nelson learned that he would referee the organization's interim featherweight title fight between Chris John and Oscar Leon, scheduled on the last night of the convention. "I had attended the convention the previous year and given my résumé to WBA President Gilberto Mendoza," said Nelson. "When I went to the '03 convention I didn't know there was a fight on the schedule. I didn't have my referee shoes or attire with me, but was able to borrow some from a referee I knew from Panama. The clothes were a bit baggy. And I stuffed Kleenex in the shoes to make them feel better, but I was more concerned about doing a good job in the title fight than my wardrobe, especially with Señor Mendoza, other WBA officers, and many of the world's top referees sitting at ringside.

"It couldn't have worked out better, though," he said. "The fight went the full twelve rounds and there were no problems. Less than two months later the WBA sent me to South Korea for another title fight, and my relationship with the WBA has been great ever since."

In Wisconsin, Nelson has refereed all the bouts on a card. Once in Stuggart, Germany, he worked back-to-back twelve-round title fights. The other extreme for Nelson was the night he was assigned to Cardiff, Wales, to work a bout televised on the Showtime cable network. "I went to Wales to referee Joe Calzaghe and that fight only lasted ninety seconds," he said. "I would much rather work two fights that go the distance than one fight that lasts ninety seconds of work. That's a long way to travel for ninety seconds!"

Fitness is an important component of his job, and to make sure he's up to snuff, Nelson does regular roadwork and punches the heavy bag. "At times, the twelve-rounders may actually be easier to work than the four-, six-, and eight-round contests," he indicated. "The championship boxers usually are more fluid and require less breaking up."

When he does have to break them up, Nelson makes sure to loudly proclaim his intention to prevent a recurrence of what happened when he failed to do so during a nationally-televised fight between Roger Mayweather and Patrick Byrd. "I went in to separate them without using the command 'Break!'" recalled Nelson. "Just as I was moving in, Mayweather decided to punch out on his own and blasted a hook that hit me solidly in the chest. It winded me for a little bit, but I was OK. Since then I have never tried to separate fighters without calling, 'Break!'"

Sometimes a plum overseas assignment doesn't pan out. That was the case when Nelson received a voicemail notifying him that he'd been selected to work an International Boxing Federation heavyweight title elimination match in Tashkent, Uzbekistan, scheduled for September 21, 2001. The message came on September 10, and "when I called back early the next morning to accept I couldn't get through to the IBF offices because its phones were dead," he said. "Then I turned on the morning news and found out about what had just happened at the World Trade Center. After I spoke with someone at the U.S. State Department I decided not to do the fight. I don't like to turn down assignments abroad, but with everything going on here I thought it best to sit this one out."

In late 2010, Nelson got the call to referee his first world heavyweight title contest, between Wladimir Klitschko and Dereck Chisora for the IBF, WBO, and IBO belts in Mannheim, Germany. But as he was in Detroit boarding a flight for Germany, Mark got word on his Blackberry that the fight had been called off because Klitschko was injured during a public workout. One hour later, Nelson was on his way back to Minneapolis.

Outside the boxing world Nelson is a senior print operator and owns his own custom picture framing business. He pictures himself involved in boxing for as long as he's able.

"It's been a tremendous experience," he said. "Sometimes you make decisions that people don't like or agree with, so you have to acquire thick skin. But I have visited some great places and formed friendships with many wonderful people around the world. It has been a great and fulfilling career, and I can't wait to see what lies ahead."

18

Randy Neumann

P ast heavyweight champions and contenders rarely return to the ring as referees. Heavyweight greats Joe Louis, Rocky Marciano, and Jersey Joe Walcott, along with title challenger Ron Stander, turned to refereeing after their fighting days were over, but none had the success or longevity of Randy Neumann, a contender in the 1970s when the division was filled with historic names like Ali, Frazier, Norton and Foreman.

He retired in 1977, with a record of 31-7, and had once been ranked ninth in the world. Neumann had held the New Jersey heavyweight title and had three memorable contests with fellow Jersey resident and contender Chuck "Bayonne Bleeder" Wepner.

Their third fight was in 1974 at Madison Square Garden. The winner was promised a shot against champion Muhammad Ali.

The audience should've been issued ponchos at the door to shield them from the splattering blood. That was the norm when Wepner fought, as he was known for bleeding. This time, however, Neumann was bleeding heavily as well from a cut over his left eye, opened when the fighters banged heads in the sixth round.

"Blood was flying everywhere," recalled Neumann in an interview with the authors, "and referee Arthur Mercante said he was going to stop the fight. Wepner pleaded with him, 'You can't stop it! I've got a shot at the heavyweight title riding on this!'

"'It isn't your blood this time,' Mercante told him. 'It's Neumann's!'

"'Well, then you should stop the fight,' Wepner hastily said. 'That's a bad cut!'"

Mercante stopped it, and Wepner went on to fight Ali in 1975. Ali won in the fifteenth round on a technical knockout, but Wepner's courageous effort gave Sylvester Stallone the idea to write a film script about a long-shot heavyweight title challenger. It became the blockbuster movie *Rocky*, which was anointed Best Picture in the 1976 Academy Awards and spawned six popular sequels.

"If I didn't get cut in the sixth round of that fight with Chuck," joked Neumann, "there would have been no *Rocky*."

At that time, New Jersey was one of the few places where instead of having ringside judges score a fight and declare the winner, the referee was solely responsible for deciding who won. In Neumann's second bout with Wepner, in 1972, Neumann and "ten of the eleven newspapermen covering the fight thought he had won hands down," according to Neumann. But the referee gave the decision to Wepner. Before his comeback fight against Ibar Arrington on April 15, 1977, Neumann successfully petitioned to have qualified judges do the scoring. It's been that way ever since, and the credit he got for that major reform was Neumann's consolation prize after Arrington stopped him on cuts in the fifth round.

When Neumann took his paycheck for the fight to the bank, it bounced. He went to the promoter for a new check, and vowed that if this one didn't clear he would come back and bounce the promoter. The new check cleared, and Neumann decided to quit boxing while he was ahead.

As a high school student in Paramus, New Jersey, Neumann competed in wrestling and football. Upon graduation he went to New York to study at the New York Institute of Technology. After classes he usually headed to a nearby YMCA to keep in shape, and it was there he was introduced to boxing. He liked it immediately. In 1967 he got serious about the sport and started going to the legendary Gleason's Gym in the Bronx, training headquarters of innumerable ring greats.

It was an atmosphere unlike any he'd ever been in before. "One day on my way into the gym I saw Mr. Gleason kick a bum down two flights of stairs," Neumann recalled. "Gleason's eventually became the best office I ever had. I loved training there. Great fighters like Emile Griffith, Carlos Ortiz, and Edwin and Adolfo Viruet trained there when I started.It was the premier gym in New York City for aspiring boxers like me, as long as you stayed on the good side of Bobby Gleason."

His first pro fight was at historic Madison Square Garden in 1969, and Neumann made a little history there himself. Fighting in an early preliminary match on a card headlined by George Foreman, Randy knocked down his opponent, Jeff Marx, with a right cross with just two seconds remaining in the first round. It was the very first time that, under a new rule just adopted by the New York boxing commission, a fighter could not be "saved by the bell." The referee's count continued after the bell, and Neumann was credited with a first-round knockout.

Neumann would fight eleven more times at the Garden, including main events. After his retirement as a boxer, Neumann went to Fairleigh Dickinson University and earned a degree in business. Today he runs a successful financial planning business in Paramus.

Several years after his final fight Neumann decided he would like to give refereeing a try. He contacted John Condon, president of Madison Square Garden Boxing, and asked him to put in a good word for him with the boxing commission. After serving an apprenticeship in preliminary bouts, he wore his bowtie to the big time.

The responsibilities of a referee have changed plenty since the days when Neumann started out.

"When I was boxing, a referee's main role was to stay out of the way of a fight in progress and count to ten if a boxer was knocked down," he said. "Today, referees attend medical seminars, hold a rules meeting before the fight, and supervise both corners during it."

In the old days, "if you came back to the corner a little groggy, you got a whiff of smelling salts from your handler to bring you to your senses," he recalled of his personal experience in the ring. Today, smelling salts aren't allowed in corners because they're a stimulant used to override the body's warnings of pain.

"Years ago, I attended a medical conference where the subject of smelling salts came up," said Neumann. "When I asked Dr. Bennet Derby, a professor of clinical neurology and pathology at New York University, why he thought smelling salts were so bad, he said, 'How would you feel if I pushed a fork up your nose?'"

Other changes in recent decades include what a cornerman can use to stem the bleeding of his boxer's cut. "When I was fighting," said Neumann, "some handlers mixed an iron-based powder with Vaseline, creating a solution that would stop the bleeding even if your head was cut off at the neck! This solution very effectively stopped cuts around the eye, but it had some dangerous side effects. For instance, if it got into the boxer's cornea, blindness could be the result. Furthermore, if a physician stitched up the cut after the fight without digging out the solution beforehand, the residue would harden and leave hard, rock-like protuberances around your eyes. A boxer would then literally have rocks in his head and this could make him more susceptible to cuts in his next contest."

Dr. Derby also taught Neumann how to detect when a concussion has occurred during a bout. "He explained that a concussion, just like a fainting spell, is a short circuit to the brain's electrical impulses, and in most cases is a brief neurological episode that leaves no long-term harm," Neumann recalled. "At the seminar, Dr. Derby asked us, 'If I turned the lights off and then back on ten seconds later, what could happen?' The answer was probably nothing in such a short time. But, he said, if the lights were out long enough for everybody to get up and start running around in the dark, chances were good that somebody would be hurt.

"The same is true of a concussion in the ring. If a boxer is injured, knocked down, and cannot continue before the count of ten, the fight is over and as referees we inspect the losing fighter and rarely find any damage," he explained. "But tragic problems may arise when a fighter receives a concussion that goes undetected and over the course of the fight his condition worsens. Then you end up with a damaged boxer in your ring."

A fighter can suffer a concussion without being knocked out. Neumann has been trained to look for "soft signs" that may signal a concussion.

"Just because a boxer is still on his feet and throwing punches does not mean he is necessarily OK," he said. "They are programmed from all of their training to punch in their sleep. So you keep an eye out for lots of things. For example, it could be the difference in which a fighter reacts to getting hit. Perhaps he covered up earlier, but doesn't now. It could be in his gait, or the way he throws punches. It could be anything that looks different. As a referee, I need to be able to detect these soft signs.

"When a fighter is knocked down and his eyes roll up in his head that is a clear sign of a concussion that every referee would easily identify. But it's the more subtle signs we have to look out for, because these are human lives in our hands."

In 1989, undefeated heavyweight champion Mike Tyson was blasting out challengers in spectacular fashion. When highly ranked Carl "The Truth" Williams fought Tyson on July 21 in Atlantic City, Neumann got the call to be the third man in the ring.

The contest ended in the first round when Williams stepped in with a left jab and Tyson countered with a left hook that sent the challenger to the mat. Williams got up before the count of ten, but Neumann halted the fight and was subjected to irate criticism from Williams and many watching the bout on HBO for what they considered a hasty stoppage.

Also an accomplished freelance writer, Neumann defended himself in a piece published in the *New York Times* on July 30, 1989, titled, "Truth Didn't Understand the Consequences." It pointed out several of the soft signs of concussion he had detected in Williams' behavior.

"He went down without a 'parachute reaction,'" Neumann wrote, "i.e., extending his arms to cushion the fall (soft sign). At six, he was unsteady on his feet, leaning on the ropes. Cognizant of all the evidence of concussion, I asked him the simple question, 'How are you?' Such a question is open-ended. I was not so concerned with what he had to say but how he said it. A fighter who wants to continue should be looking to convince or at least acknowledge the referee. I asked the question twice of Williams, between what would have been the count nine and ten, and when he could not, or would not, respond he gave me a very clear sign of concussion. I stopped the fight because, at the count of ten, the juice was still off."

Neumann contrasts Williams's response—or lack of one—with what happened once to Jose Torres, light heavyweight champion of the world, after he was knocked down in a fight at the Garden. Torres got up, and when asked the standard who-and-where-are you questions by the referee he responded, "I'm Jose Torres, I'm in Madison Square Garden, and this guy is beating the hell out of me!"

Refereeing has taken Neumann all over the world. "Working a title fight in a foreign country is a bit like being an out-of-town hit man for hire," he says. "You travel to the site, you are involved in some of the pre-fight activities, the rules meetings, the weigh-in; you work the fight, and then you're on your way back home. This usually all takes place within 48–72 hours."

One of his favorite assignments was in Lucca, Italy, for a world light welterweight title fight between Reyes Cruz and Gary Hinton.

The plane bound for Italy left New York at 8:30 on a Wednesday night and landed the next day in Milan. Because of terrorist bombing in Tripoli, the airport in Milan had an abundance of security, including machine gun–toting soldiers and lots of mean-looking dogs. After a long and harrowing security check-through, Neumann and the other officials connected with the fight boarded a small bus for a four-hour ride to Lucca. There they were treated like foreign dignitaries, given a hearty Italian meal, and escorted on a walking tour of the town by some local people of importance.

It was a brisk, entertaining fight that went the distance. The boxers required little direction from Neumann, and he recalls being glad that referees were no longer required to do double-duty by also acting as a judge. "I was concerned with the well-being of the boxers and enforcing the rules rather than worrying about who was ahead," he wrote in "On a Working Visit to Italy and Thoughts on Boxing," a May 25, 1986, article in the *New York Times*.

The next day, Neumann, the other officials, and the boxers and their handlers all boarded the bus for Milan. "By the time we were halfway there," he recalled in his *New York Times* article, "everyone acted like life-long friends—even the fighters themselves. To non-boxing people it might appear strange that two guys who had faced each other in heated battle the previous day were now acting like old friends. To a boxing person, though, it's not odd. The rationale is something like, 'We were at the top of the game before the fight. We shared something special during the fight. We made a few bucks. We're still at the top. Life is good.'"

As a full-time certified financial planner and successful businessman, Neumann knows the feeling of being at the top. He is a syndicated financial columnist who has also written articles for the prestigious *Forbes* magazine. Neumann is also a frequent seminar speaker and has appeared on many television shows, including MSNBC's *Moneyline*. He is especially proud to have helped the IBF set up a worldwide pension plan for boxers involved in its title fights. He is also a member of the New Jersey Boxing Hall of Fame.

19

John O'Brien

J ohn O'Brien has worn many hats, both inside and outside the boxing ring. The project funding specialist is a veteran professional boxing referee who has officiated numerous major fights, including televised matches on HBO, Showtime, ESPN, Comcast, TeleFutura, and pay-per-view. He is also the chief official of the Chicago Golden Gloves, one of the longest running and most prestigious amateur boxing tournaments in the United States (it's been in existence since 1923). O'Brien has worked in boxing as a state inspector, timekeeper, judge, coach, a professional and amateur promoter, and also as a referee in kickboxing matches. He has been refereeing amateur boxing since 1995 and professional contests since 2003.

O'Brien, a fitness fanatic who comes from a martial arts background, has a black belt in Kosho Ryu Kempo and is a former powerlifting champion. Also an outdoorsman, his other interests include hunting, fishing, hiking, and kayaking.

For O'Brien, boxing is a family affair. He still recalls sitting in a restaurant in 1971 with his father, who asked if he would be interested in watching the first Joe Frazier vs. Muhammad Ali fight on closed circuit television at western suburban Chicago's Hillside Theater. John took his father up on the offer. It was the first professional boxing match he ever watched. While the eleven-year-old-John predicted that Ali would win, it was the victorious

Frazier who won him over with his tenacity and relentless style. That year O'Brien attended the Chicago Golden Gloves with his father, John "Jack" O'Brien, an attorney. He has not missed a Golden Gloves tournament since.

In 1999, O'Brien and his father, who had previously been diagnosed with cancer, went to the doctor's office. The cancer was thought to have been beaten, but that day they learned it had not only spread, but was terminal. O'Brien was on his way to referee at the Golden Gloves that night and asked his father if he wanted to go home after he received the prognosis. His father said that he would like to watch some boxing that night, to find some solace from the bad news. They had attended every tournament together since first going in 1971. That night, a ringside photographer took a photo of the pair—it was the last photo taken of the two together. O'Brien's father, whom he called "the smartest man I have ever known," died shortly thereafter.

O'Brien's biggest focus today is being a devoted father to his two children—his son, Al, and daughter, Shelby. Family obligations have made him decline several high-profile bouts over the years for which he would have had to travel.

O'Brien's son is a college wrestler who has also done some amateur boxing and sports an unbeaten record. Al can often be seen ringside at events, both professional and amateur, around Chicago land. Shelby is a student at Michigan State University and has sung the national anthem before an ESPN show in which her father worked at Chicago's UIC Pavilion.

Preparation and organization are key for O'Brien—both in the way he conducts his daily life, and in the way he officiates a match. Before the fight, he closely observes the boxers in the locker room. Once inside the ring, he looks for the timekeeper, the cornermen, and ringside doctors. A cardinal rule is to treat every fight, from the four-rounders to twelve-round championships, as the biggest and most important match. "It may be the only time that kid fights professional," said O'Brien of the four-round fights. "It is big to him."

O'Brien credits Genaro "Geno" Rodriguez, an Illinois referee who has officiated over many world title and international bouts, for breaking him in and teaching him. Geno taught him to command respect from the fighter and his corner from the moment of pre-fight locker room instructions. O'Brien is also mindful of the advice of former Illinois boxing commissioner Sean Curtin, one of his early mentors, who warned that with a bad decision, especially on television, one's career can end in an instant. O'Brien is aware he must always be focused. He closely follows boxing, and when he does, he not only watches the boxers but also the referee. When he first became a referee, O'Brien would go over his fights with Curtin, also an experienced referee, after the match had ended. When a fight of O'Brien's is on television, he will tape it and watch it twelve to fifteen times, making sure he has made all the right moves and decisions—the same way a trainer watches tapes of fighters. "I know there is no way to be 100 percent correct, but I better be damn close," said O'Brien of his decisions in the ring.

Because of his extensive experience working with amateurs, he usually knows the styles, strengths, and flaws of the boxers he officiates in Chicago, yet he remains completely impartial. "If I am not familiar with the fighters, I do not make an effort to study or research the fighters beforehand," said O'Brien, who is usually able to make assessments about the fighters once the fight begins. He cites a 2010 fight he worked on ESPN2, between two-time Venezuelan olympian Patrick Lopez and former National Golden Glove Champion Prenice Brewer, who was undefeated at the time. While many in the press may have been touting the undefeated Brewer, "it was immediately apparent the difference in strength and punching power," recalled O'Brien. "About a minute into the fight, it became clear Brewer was going to have a hard time winning this fight. Lopez was literally lifting Brewer off the canvas with his body blows." Lopez scored a third-round technical knockout over a defenseless Brewer.

When O'Brien refereed the WBA world heavyweight title fight between the hyped seven-foot-tall titlist Nikolay Valuev and challenger Monte Barrett, he came in with no preconceived notions. Barrett was considered by many to be a fading name, far too small to give Valuev a contest. Outweighed by more than a hundred pounds—328 pounds for Valuev to 222 pounds for Barrett—the smaller man gave his all before fading late. "Barrett actually was throwing the harder punches, had better technique, and hurt Valuev several times," said O'Brien. "Over the course of time, the huge weight advantage was just too much, and Barrett wore down."

To a young aspiring referee, O'Brien suggests starting by judging younger children's junior boxing matches. The Chicago park district has an active boxing program. "Watch the fighters, watch how they move, and watch the referee, his positioning, and how he moves," he said. "Watch as much boxing as you can. Get used to the movement, and being in position. After a year or so, you may be ready to referee park district matches, which are one-minute rounds."

O'Brien is proud of his crew of officials at the Chicago Golden Gloves. The majority of them work professional boxing matches, and others were professional officials in the past. All of the professional boxing referees in Illinois work at the Chicago Golden Gloves, and while there are many amateur boxing officials in the state, only a select few are chosen for the Golden Gloves. O'Brien imposes strict attendance requirements to make sure the officials are fresh and at their best throughout the tournament. He recognizes the need for effective officiating, especially for the Chicago Golden Gloves finals, where the winners among the open division boxers, who have more experience, go on to compete in the national tournament.

O'Brien has daily pre-fight meetings at the twelve-night tournament to go over what was done well in the previous night and what can be improved. He constantly stresses the importance of the tournament to the young men and women who are boxing, as well as the potential national implications some of the matches hold.

Whether professional or amateur, O'Brien stresses the appearance of referee and judges and how they must command respect by the way they look, act, and conduct themselves. In the past, he has sent Golden Gloves officials home because they lacked the proper dress.

O'Brien has several rules that govern the way he officiates a fight. "You are not part of the show," he emphasized. "I believe that the best compliment that you can pay a referee is that you cannot remember who refereed a particular bout. I am not going to think for one second that the fans are there to see me, and interject myself into the fight. I am not one for catchy phrases in the television pre-bout instructions. My job is to let the boxers box, to monitor them, to make sure they follow the rules, and to make sure no one gets hurt. Some referees let their ego get the best of them. The crowd is not there to see the referee; they are there to watch a boxing match." Among the non-Chicago referees, he cites Steve Smoger and Benjy Esteves as two of the referees he feels stand out for their excellence and whose style he appreciates. "The more you work, the more you internalize your actions and not think before acting," said O'Brien. "Whether pro or amateur, we owe it to fighters. You don't, or should not, become pro ref to get paid."

O'Brien considers 1996 Olympian David Diaz to be one of the most impressive amateur fighters he has officiated. He also worked the amateur bouts of 1996 Olympian Nate Jones and 2000 Olympian Michael Bennett. Shane Mosley, whom he co-promoted in a 1997 match, impressed O'Brien, too. Mosley—who was 22-0 and a fight away from winning his first world title, a decision over IBF lightweight champion Philip Holiday—scored a fourth-round knockout on his card.

In the professional ranks, O'Brien has refereed many of the world's top boxers. Included among them are Erislandy Lara, Danny Jacobs, Montell Griffin, Brandon Rios, Giovanni Segura, Miguel Acosta, Orlando Salido, Librado Andrade, Marco Antonio Rubio, Ricardo Castillo, Guillermo Jones, Steve Luevano, Demetrius Hopkins, and Arthur Johnson.

Among the biggest and best matches he has worked are the battle between future IBF light heavyweight champion Tavoris Cloud and former world titlist Julio Gonzalez for the IBF light heavyweight title eliminator, Martin Honorio vs. Rogers Mtagwa for the NABF featherweight title, Nikolay Valuev vs. Monte Barrett for the WBA world heavyweight title, Luis Collazo against former champion Miguel Angel Gonzalez for the WBA welterweight title, and Israel Vazquez against Armando Guerrero for the IBF super bantamweight title.

One of O'Brien's favorite matches was a war in 2007 between two Chicago fighters—the former outstanding Chicago Golden Gloves boxer, a much-hyped prospect Louis Turner, 11-0, against Angel Hernandez, 27-6, former NABF junior middleweight champion and world title challenger. O'Brien was familiar with both fighters, having refereed them since their amateur days. Hernandez was thought to have his best years behind him, and had not fought in almost a year and a half. In a toe-to-toe slugfest and an upset, Hernandez won a hard-fought unanimous decision.

O'Brien stands as an example of how meticulous preparation, readiness, and organization pay off as a referee. His success is due in part to self-analysis. He practices what he preaches, constantly working on his skills, justifiably projecting confidence, and internalizing his decisions. These are the qualities that enable him to stand out as one of boxing's best referees.

20

Luis Pabon

Luis Pabon is one of boxing's most experienced officials, having worked well over a hundred title fights. He was the youngest official to ever attain such a lofty number, working his one hundredth title bout at the age of forty-four. He is the chief official of the WBA, a title he has held since 2009. As chief official, he is responsible for overseeing and training numerous world class officials.

Many would be surprised to find out that Pabon learned how to referee and judge fights by answering an ad—in the Yellow Pages! When he was twenty-five, Pabon wanted to participate in boxing but was not sure whom to call. So he called up the Puerto Rican Boxing Federation. He scheduled an appointment, and the rest is history.

Pabon met with the federation and shortly after was learning the art of judging and refereeing and officiating amateur bouts. He participated in an amateur tournament in the Dominican Republic and in 1991, after some additional amateur experience, turned professional. By 1993, he had judged his first world title fight, and he refereed his first world title fight in 1994—John John Molina and Wilson Rodriguez for the IBF super featherweight title.

Pabon is from the boxing-rich island of Puerto Rico—home of Wilfredo Gomez, Carlos Ortiz, Wilfred Benitez, Juan Manuel Lopez, Miguel Cotto, and Felix Trinidad—where boxing is still a major sport. "Boxing is very popular in Puerto Rico. There have been more than sixty world champions from here," stated Pabon, who has refereed fights involving Cotto, Trinidad, and Lopez. Yet, working the fights of national heroes does not faze him. "I feel some tension in refereeing a good fight, but I do not get nervous about who the fighters are. They can be big name fighters or newcomers. I just want to referee or judge a good fight."

Like many of boxing's top officials, Pabon is a student of the game and is always working to better his skills. "I am always analyzing a fight, the referee, and the fighters. I am always learning from the good and the bad." Pabon has been married for twenty-four years as of this writing and has four daughters, ranging in age from twenty-one to nine-year-old twin daughters. He is a supervisor in a manufacturing plant in Puerto Rico's capital city, San Juan, and he lives in Bayamon. Pabon has long been an avid runner and a cyclist. Several years ago, he participated in his first triathlon and has since completed several more.

Pabon has refereed fights in Japan, Thailand, Australia, the United States, and throughout Europe. He has refereed such major bouts as Andre Ward vs. Arthur Abraham in Showtime's "Super Six" Middleweight tournament, Nikolay Valuev vs. Evander Holyfield, Virgil Hill vs. Fabrice Tiozzo, and Juan Manuel Marquez vs. Derrick Gainer. He was a judge in "Prince" Naseem Hamed vs. Augie Sanchez and Alexander Povetkin vs. Chris Byrd. He has refereed matches involving Amir Khan, David Haye, Giovanni Segura, Ivan Calderon, Juan Manuel Lopez, Edwin Valero, Michael Moorer, Ruslan Chagaev, Koki Kameda, Shannon Briggs, Mikkel Kessler, Chris John, Wladimir Klitschko, Simon Brown, and Julian Jackson. "One of my two most important rules is that the boxers, not the officials, are the stars," explained Pabon. "Many officials want to be the star. That is not why we are there. The second rule, and just as important, are the pre-fight instructions in the dressing room. You have to give the fighter specific instructions. You want to gain the respect of the boxers. Once they come to the ring, and get in it, you do not want to be fighting with the boxer. It is what you do in the dressing room that keeps this from happening."

He cites the Nikolay Valuev vs. Evander Holyfield fight as an example of pre-fight instructions paying dividends. The fight was for Valuev's WBA heavyweight title on December 20, 2008, in Zurich, Switzerland. Valuev won by majority decision. "In the dressing room, I saw Holyfield," Pabon recalled. "He is older than me, and has been a great champion. In some fights, he had a reputation for committing fouls. I let him know that it was an honor, and that I had respect for him. But in the ring, he would have to respect me, and respect the ring. He told me 'Don't worry. I'm a gentleman.' And they had a good fight, a clean fight. I had no problems. There was respect at all times."

True to his nature of trying to learn, better himself, and strive for perfection, Pabon's most memorable fights were also learning experiences. "One of the best fights for me was Freddie Norwood and Antonio Cermeno," he said, recalling the May 29, 1999, bout at the Roberto Clemente Coliseum. "Everyone told me it was going to be a dirty fight. Norwood was very good, but he fought dirty." Norwood won a decision in a rough battle. Some had told Pabon he might not be ready to work a fight with boxers who might frequently foul. Pabon admits he has learned a great deal about refereeing since then, and has improved greatly because of educational bouts like this one. Another memorable fight was the November 1, 2003, contest between Juan Manuel Marquez and Derrick Gainer. The WBA and IBF featherweight title unification fight was held in Grand Rapids, Michigan, on the Floyd Mayweather vs. Phillip N'Dou card, and televised by HBO. Fighting was stopped in the seventh-round when a gash by Gainer's left eye began bleeding heavily. Pabon ruled that the cut was caused by an unintentional head butt by Marquez. Others initially criticized Pabon, saying the cut was caused by a Marquez punch. If the cut had been caused by a Marquez punch, the fight would have ended as a technical knockout win for Marquez.

"I ruled that it was a butt that caused the cut on Gainer. So we went to the scorecards, to a decision. Marquez won on the scorecards," said Pabon. "The replay showed that my call was correct, it was a head butt." Intense focus and concentration is necessary for a referee. In this fight for Marquez's WBA title and Gainer's IBF title, Pabon proved that he had the necessary level of attention to make these difficult split-second calls.

In May 2011, Andre Ward, the WBA champion and number one rated super middleweight in the world according to *The Ring* magazine, was scheduled to fight German-based former IBF middleweight champion Arthur Abraham. The fight was part of Showtime's prestigious "Super Six" tournament, which featured the top super middleweight fighters in the world. The location of the match was in Carson, California in Ward's home state. The original referee selected for the match-up was a very capable official from California. Abraham was facing elimination after losing two fights in the tournament, and his camp objected to the use of a Californian referee, fearing favoritism. Pabon was brought in to officiate over the contest instead. His assignment drew no objection from Ward, Abraham, or their respective handlers. The fight went off without incident, and Ward won a twelve-round decision, moving to the Super Six finals, and eventually winning the tournament.

All in all, quite an officiating career from a man who first learned the art by looking through the Yellow Pages. Experienced Chicago professional boxing judge Ted Gimza noted, "I have had the pleasure of working with Luis on several occasions. It is obvious that he takes his responsibility seriously.

"Good referees need to not only have physical coordination and stamina," Gimza continued. "They also need to have intestinal fortitude, the ability to make a split second decision under pressure, and the compassion to know when 'enough is enough.' Remember, all these things must be present at the same time, and often under the scrutiny of bright lights, local commissions, television analysts, sanctioning bodies, and what might be the most difficult at times—the boxers, their corners, managers, and promoters. This is definitely not a job that anyone can handle! Luis does, and he does it well. He is among the best that I've seen."

21

Carlos Padilla

For many sports fans worldwide, their introduction to Carlos "Sonny" Padilla Jr. was on October 1, 1975. That was the date of the third fight in the Muhammad Ali vs. Joe Frazier trilogy, the "Thrilla in Manilla." Ali won the match at the end of the fourteenth round when Frazier's trainer, the great Eddie Futch, did not allow "Smokin' Joe" to answer the bell for the final round. In 1996, the fight was selected by *The Ring* magazine as the number one greatest title fight of all-time. *Time* also rated the fight as the best boxing match of all time, and *Sports Illustrated* ranked it second only to the 1923 fight between Jack Dempsey and Luis Firpo.

As the fight was in the Philippines, Filipino president Ferdinand Marcos wanted a local referee. At the time, Padilla had been refereeing for ten years but had never worked a fight anywhere near this magnitude. Padilla was chosen as the referee for the fight, though he was previously unknown in international circles.

Padilla, however, was well-known in the Philippines. He was a childhood actor from a very prominent family. His father, Carlos Padilla Sr., was a leading man in movies as well as an Olympic boxer. His uncle, Jose, was an actor as well. Carlos Padilla Jr., the referee, is the father of well-known actress and singer Esperanza "Zsa Zsa" Padilla.

Padilla and two other Filipinos were in the running for the honor to referee the Ali vs. Frazier fight. According to Padilla, "I found out the day of the fight. I set out to see and get in the ring with my uncle, who was a former boxer and an actor, at 6 a.m. I was told 'don't be afraid.' As an actor, I was used to the lights."

When he got to the venue, Padilla was surprised by the size of the ring. "It was a big ring," he recalled. "We have mainly small fighters in the Philippines. I could not believe the size. We usually referee flyweights, bantamweights, and featherweights."

Frazier had won the first meeting. Ali won the second. The third fight was a war. It was a very physical fight, and neither fighter was ever the same thereafter. Following the fight, Padilla recalled, "I had to pull the fighters, and my feet were blistered. My hands hurt. I am only 5'8", 160 pounds, and those were big, powerful men."

Padilla did distinguish Joe Frazier from many current fighters, who Padilla believes fight dirty. "Frazier was one of the cleanest fighters. He just came forward, and kept hitting you."

When refereeing a fighter in a match who had fouled his opponent, Padilla noted, "I would see little things right away, not let it pass, and give a warning. [In the past] a low blow could do a lot of damage, the cups were loose to the balls. That was before they were made to order, before they fit." Padilla was never a referee that was eager, or "trigger happy" as he called it, to stop fights. "When someone was hurt, or groggy, I would put myself in his shoes, and ask 'can I recover,'" he said. "That is boxing—you don't immediately stop the fight."

He was also one of the first referees to use a mandatory eight count after a knockdown. "I would stand three feet away, and ask 'are you OK?' If they did not answer, I would stop the fight," said Padilla. "If they did answer, I would say 'come, give me the gloves' [to wipe the gloves off]. If they walked and wobbled, then that's enough." Padilla believes that his acting experience was helpful in preparing him for work as a referee. "When you are used to facing the cameras and the lights, it is an advantage," he said. "Before a take, you rehearse. You go through preparation in your mind. Refereeing is like filming a movie."

In the late 1970s, he moved to Las Vegas, to "do the big fights, and to try my luck."

"I came in to apply to be a referee," recalled Padilla. "They said 'he's good,' but that they only had spots for seven referees. But they had boxing every week at the Silver Slipper [a hotel/casino that held weekly fight cards on the strip]. I was denied at first. I had to come in and show them magazines that had me as boxing's 'referee of the year' before I got licensed."

The one-time leading man and top referee in the Philippine Islands had to work many different jobs to support himself while lobbying to become a referee in Nevada. "I worked all kinds of jobs," he said. "I never thought I would be working in jobs like this. I grew up rich. I was head bus boy, bar boy. I bought a book, and learned how to tend bar. I tended bar at Caesars Palace. I worked as a dealer in a lot of little places. There are a lot of Philippine people that work in these jobs."

Eventually Padilla did enjoy a sensational career as an international referee. He officiated many blockbuster fights, including Ray Leonard vs. Wilfred Benitez, Mike Tyson vs. Pinklon Thomas, Roberto Duran vs. Sugar Ray Leonard I, Thomas Hearns vs. Roberto Duran, Dwight Muhammad Qawi vs. Mathew Saad Muhammad, George Foreman vs. Dwight Muhammad Qawi, Salvador Sanchez vs. Wilfredo Gomez, Julio Cesar Chavez vs. Terrance Alli, Michael Spinks vs. Larry Holmes I, Greg Haugen vs. Hector Camacho, Nigel Benn vs. Iran Barkley, George Foreman vs. Adilson Rodriguez, Jorge Paez vs. Troy Dorsey I, Michael Nunn vs. Iran Barkley, and Bobby Chacon vs. Cornelius Boza Edwards II. Padilla also was the third man for bouts involving Azumah Nelson, Jung Koo Chang, Donald Curry, Evander Holyfield, Meldrick Taylor, John Mugabi, Danny Lopez, Ken Norton, Alexis Arguello, Marvin Hagler, and Lupe Pintor.

"I remember Sugar Ray Leonard against Wilfred Benitez," said Padilla of the 1979 fight held at Caesars Palace. "Leonard was the Olympic gold medalist, and this was his first world title shot. Benitez, he had been champion for a while, but he was the youngest boxing champion in history [Benitez was twenty-one at the time of the fight and undefeated, but had been a world champion since the age of seventeen]. I stopped the fight with about [six] seconds left to go. But I got no complaints. Benitez went down, and when he got up, he was hurt bad. My job is the safety of the boxers—not a timekeeper.

"I came to the United States to referee fights," explained Padilla. "Many people would want to talk to me about boxing, to meet me. Especially after the boxing matches. I would get invited to a lot of parties. But I did not go to the parties, and I did not mingle. After the fight I would just go home."

Throughout his career, he always stayed in condition. "I would jog, do boxing exercises, the speed bag, and jump rope. I would train like a boxer—except not spar. I believed in sound mind and sound body. A referee cannot afford to make a mistake. For example, if I had made a mistake in the Ali vs. Frazier fight, they would have burned the place!"

The last fight Padilla ever refereed was Manny Pacquiao vs. Nedal Hussein in October of 2001. "Every time I went to the Philippines, people always wanted me to referee the fights, and especially Manny's fights," Padilla said. "That was before Manny had come to the United States, but he was very popular in the Philippines. He got knocked down in the fourth round by Hussein, who was trained by Jeff Fenech. But he came back to win." Ironically, Padilla also refereed two fights of Pacquiao's Hall of Fame trainer, Freddie Roach, in the 1980s in Las Vegas.

Padilla retired as a boxing referee in 2001. He says the reason he retired was "Politics. I no longer got the big fights. So I retired and never looked back."

Since retiring, Padilla indicated that he had only been to one fight. "I went to the Manny Pacquiao vs. Oscar De La Hoya fight," he said of the December 6, 2008, "passing of the torch" fight where Pacquiao moved up in weight to stop and retire boxing's biggest gate attraction, De La Hoya. "My granddaughter, Karylle, sang the Philippine national anthem before the fight. She is Zsa Zsa's daughter, and she had dedicated her performance to me. I came to see her."

Today, while no longer involved in boxing, Padilla continues to work. He is an aide at Harmon Hospital in Las Vegas, working the afternoon shift transporting patients. "When I am not working, it is like a taxi that's meter is down. Every time I don't work, on days off, I envy those who work. I get bored, and there is no income," said the active Padilla. "I still work out regularly, too. I do the chin up bar every other day. I shadow box, I do the speed bag, I hit the bags, and I jog." Padilla says that his family always tells him, "Papa, stop working," but the third man for the "Thrilla in Manila" is still going strong.

22

Pete Podgorski

"Growing up in Chicago, for us, it was a big deal to go to Wisconsin," said veteran Chicago referee Pete Podgorski. Thanks to the sweet science, however, Podgorski has traveled all around the United States, as well as to the Netherlands, Australia, Denmark, Canada, Colombia, England, Northern Ireland, France, Germany, Italy, Ireland, Mexico, Panama, the Philippines, Poland, and South Africa.

The hard-working former professional boxer, with a 22-15 (16 KO's) record, is a retired park supervisor of recreation, having worked for the Chicago Park District from 1975–2004. He also worked for twenty-two years as a physical education teacher at Catholic grade schools for the Archdiocese of Chicago, before retiring in 2010.

As a professional referee, Podgorski was third man in the ring for the likes of Montell Griffin, Michael Carbajal, Iran Barkley, Glen Johnson, Vic Darchinyan, Nonito Donaire, Tavoris Cloud, Orlando Salido, John Ruiz, Arthur Abraham, David Diaz, Nate Campbell, Sven Ottke, Henry Maske, James Toney, Andrew Golota, James "Bonecrusher" Smith, Meldrick Taylor, Carlos Baldomir, Angel Manfredy, Lupe Pintor, Carlos De Leon, and Raul Marquez. He also judged fights involving Cristian Mijares, Kostya Tszyu, Kennedy McKinney, and Orlando Canizales, as well as important matches such as Shane Mosley vs. Golden Johnson, Brian Nielsen vs. Larry Holmes, and an all-Chicago matchup of former cruiserweight titlists in LeRoy Murphy vs. Alfonso Ratliff.

Podgorski played baseball growing up, and was also on the track and wrestling teams in high school and he still officiates softball, baseball, and basketball games. However, it was in boxing that he made his mark. Chicago has long had a thriving amateur boxing scene, and Podgorski won the Catholic Youth Organization (CYO) novice title in 1972 and the Chicago Park District open championship in 1977. By that point, he was already a Park District employee and had begun working as a referee in Park District bouts himself. An amateur career highlight was a win (against two losses) versus future world lightweight title challenger Johnny Lira. Podgorski turned professional in 1977. Podgorski was a solid professional, a workman who gave a tough effort—the type who would give his best, but never reach contender status, often taking fights on short notice and without proper training. "Boxing is not a sport you can usually do as a part-time job," he reflected of his boxing career. "But I did it while I worked full-time with the Chicago Park District, and while I was also officiating softball and basketball on the weekend. It made for a busy schedule. I boxed mostly because it kept me close to the sport, and made me a few extra dollars. It also gave me . . . insight on professional boxing, which helped me as an official in years to come."

In one five day stretch in 1982, Podgorski, who was 7-2 at the time, fought twice against future title challengers. He was offered a fight on October 2, 1982, against future two-time world title challenger Ronnie Shields, who later gained fame as one of boxing's most respected trainers. Shields was the number ten ranked fighter at 140 pounds according to *The Ring* magazine at the time. Podgorski, who had not fought in over nine months, took a warm-up match first.

The warm-up was on Tuesday, September 28, in Indiana. Podgorski was matched against a then little-known fighter from South Bend, Indiana, named Harold Brazier, who was 6-2. Brazier won a six-round majority decision over Podgorski. Few would have predicted it, but Brazier went on to a career record of 105-18-1 (64 KOs), which would include two world title fights and stints as both the North American Boxing Federation (NABF) and United States Boxing Association (USBA) champion.

Podgorski came out of the fight with badly bruised ribs. On Saturday, he was in Atlantic City fighting Ronnie Shields on the undercard of the nationally televised, Don King–promoted Renaldo Snipes vs. Trevor Berbick fight. He was stopped with a body shot in two rounds by Shields. When asked why he fought Shields so soon after a loss, with bruised ribs, Podgorski replied, "For the money. It was a couple thousand dollars. That was a lot of money back in those days."

One of Podgorski's biggest honors was fighting on a Muhammad Ali exhibition undercard. In February of 1979, Ali fought an exhibition against local Chicago light heavyweight Luke Capuano at DePaul University's Alumni Hall. Podgorski fought and won a four round decision that night. One of Podgorski's wildest fights was a match with veteran Tom Tarantino in Milwaukee. Tarantino was a roofer and local tough guy. "He had sold a couple hundred tickets. People were drinking, and in the second round, they started throwing things. One guy tried to climb into the ring. [Another] guy had to kick him to keep him out. The bout, the final of the night, was called off. It was declared a no contest," recalled Podgorski. "But I got paid. I think it was four hundred dollars."

Podgorski came from a boxing family. His brothers Stan and Leo were boxers, and his sons ended up fighting as well. His son Matthew, a former Park District champion, is also a professional boxing referee and judge. Podgorski's wife is a Chicago police officer.

With boxing deep in his roots, when it came time to retire from boxing in 1986, Podgorski did not want to leave the sport. He had already been an amateur referee and by then, he was also a fixture across the Midwest, working as a judge in Illinois, Indiana, Wisconsin, and Iowa. To this day, Podgorski stays close to his roots, often working amateur shows, including the Chicago Golden Gloves. Podgorski's first fight as a professional referee was a four-round bout between heavyweight Kimmuel Odum and Stan Johnson on February 17, 1987. Odum was a former Chicago Golden Gloves winner who had previously won an amateur bout via disqualification against Mike Tyson. With a first-round knockout, Odum beat the infamous Stan Johnson, a heavyweight who would retire with a 4-40 record, who operated a stable of traveling losers out of

Milwaukee. Odum won by first-round knockout in Podgorski's refereeing debut.

In time, Podgorski established himself as one of the top referees in the Midwest and then worked his way up to the international and championship level. Along the way, Podgorski has had his share of odd adventures. He refereed several fights involving one of boxing's most celebrated losers, Reggie Strickland. Strickland has been featured on HBO's *Real Sports* and has been the subject of numerous magazine and newspaper articles. He retired with a listed record of 66-276-17 (14 KOs), but was only stopped in a small fraction of those bouts. With all fighters, and in all fights, Podgorski has always been a big believer in pre-fight instructions. "I tell a boxer in the dressing room, if you get knocked down, show me you want to continue. If you don't show me, I am going to stop it." In one Reggie Strickland fight, Strickland was knocked down. When he got up, Podgorski asked him if he wanted to continue. Strickland shook his head yes, indicating that he did want to fight, but he told Podgorski, "Hell, no—no I don't want to fight." Podgorski stopped the fight. The crowd went crazy, thinking that he had terminated the bout with the boxer up and willing to continue. After the match, Podgorski went up to Strickland and said "don't ever do that again." The legendary loser just smiled.

Podgorski stated that one of the first questions people typically ask boxing referees is, "did you referee Tyson," referring to Mike Tyson. Podgorski said, "Usually I just say no, but sometimes I'll smile and say 'Yeah, I refereed Michael Tyson when he fought Bobby Hitz.'" The Mike Tyson that Podgorski refereed was not "the" Mike Tyson, rather a journeyman heavyweight from Iowa named Mike Tyson who retired with a record of zero wins, seven losses. "Iowa" Mike Tyson lost a six-round decision in 1988 to a Chicago heavyweight named Robert Hitzelberger, also known as Bobby Hitz, who was a boxer with a 15-5 record and later became a Chicago promoter. Podgorski also refereed "Iowa" Mike Tyson's match against Kimmuel Odum two months later.

Podgorski relates another odd experience he had refereeing a 1996 fight between Danish heavyweight Brian Nielsen and former heavyweight contender, Mike "The Bounty" Hunter. The fight was held in Copen-hagen, Denmark.

"Neilsen was 27-0 at the time. He had a few solid victories over some big name heavyweights like Tony Tubbs and Bonecrusher Smith," recalled Podgorski. "Hunter had wins over Dwight Muhammad Qawi, Pinklon Thomas, Tyrell Biggs, Oliver McCall, and Jimmy Thunder, but was sup-posed to have had problems with drugs, and had a 1993 win over Buster Mathis Jr. ruled a no-contest, which was the result of his failing a post-fight drug test. Hunter was a bit loud and odd in the dressing room before the fight, but even more odd during the bout. He ran, he slapped, and he talked. I gave him a few cautions, but they were no-harm fouls, and they just made for a non-appealing fight. The bout lasted five rounds. Hunter was sent to the canvas, he got up, but took punishment before I stopped what was a one-sided affair.

"Even odder though, was my trip home," continued Podgorski. "I ended up being on the same flight with Mr. Hunter, only a few rows away. He made a few comments when I had to pass him up to get my seat. He was making comments like 'I can take a punch,' and 'I'm gonna come back.' I ignored him and went to my seat, but much of the long trip I could hear him talking quietly—but only to himself. It was if he was having a conver-sation with someone, but it was just him talking to himself. It was really weird as if he was singing to music with a headphone on, but there were no headphones on his head. Finally, after few hours, he fell asleep. As far as I know, Hunter never fought again. I did not hear anything of him again until 2006, when I read that 'The Bounty Hunter' was shot in an alterca-tion with police officers."

It has been quite a journey for the Chicago referee, who has maximized his experience in boxing and traveled around the world. He is always hon-ing his craft, studying and researching boxing, and awaiting his next assign-ment. His son Matthew stated, "As far as I can remember, my father has always had a real passion for boxing. As referee, he is a perfectionist. That, more than anything, has influenced me and helped me understand what it is to truly have a craft—something that you love, but are never satisfied with, because of that drive for perfection."

23

Roberto Ramirez

As impressive as Roberto Ramirez's work in the ring has been, a glimpse at his life outside the ropes enables one to see how he stays so strong at his age. He is known for working out daily and eating only the healthiest foods. He has always treated his body like a temple, and it has paid off for him as he remains in top form at age seventy-plus and after more than fifty years as a top-flight boxing referee.

Ramirez's refereeing started after he enlisted in the U.S. Army's 82nd Airborne Division. He was initially assigned to Fort Bragg, in North Carolina, and then went to Germany.

"I grew up in the tropical climate of San Juan, Puerto Rico, and when I arrived in Germany it was cold outside," he recalled. "So to stay indoors I took up the sport of boxing. I competed as an amateur boxer and also started refereeing in the Army."

After leaving active duty in 1964, Ramirez returned to San Juan and studied Economics at the University of Puerto Rico, where he obtained his masters in public administration. The studying habit he picked up there has stuck with him his whole life. "Study is the only way to keep the mind working as a machine," he said. "It's like oil to the brain."

During his college days Ramirez also applied for a license to judge and referee professional boxing in Puerto Rico.

"Boxing has changed so much since I started out," he said. "When I was invited to Texas to referee the world welterweight championship fight between Donald Curry and Jun-Suk Hwang on February 13, 1983, it was a scheduled fifteen-round contest and I acted as the referee and also scored the fight. Today there are no bouts scheduled for fifteen rounds, and referees no longer score fights. I think this is a good thing. I am glad that I no longer score the fights I am refereeing. Those are two different responsibilities. Judges look for the amount of punches landed in the scoring zone, while the referee's main responsibility is the health of the two boxers and enforcing the rules.

"For referees, to stay on top of their game, they need to continually practice. I want to make sure that no boxer in my ring receives any unnecessary punishment. This is easy to say, but it takes expert timing and hard work," Ramirez continued. "Lately, it seems that several of the world's top referees have been involved in controversy due to their judgment calls in major title fights. Years ago it seemed there was more latitude given to the referee for their decisions. Then nobody seemed to challenge a referee's judgment as frequently as they do today. Our best referees have worked hard to make it to the top, but it's staying at the top that also requires a lot of work. Once a commission or sanctioning organization has put its trust in us as a referee, we need to have the ability to instinctively react in the heat of battle. It is as basic for us as a boxer's jab. This comes from studying and practicing the rules in preparing oneself for the many circumstances that can occur in a boxing match." Ramirez has been the third man for bouts involving greats like Alexis Arguello, Aaron Pryor, "Prince" Naseem Hamed, and Juan Manuel Lopez. He has also had an impressive résumé as a boxing judge. In 1976 he judged the historic contest between Antonio Cervantes and Wilfred Benitez. In the bout, Benitez, who was undefeated and only seventeen years old, won the WBA light welterweight title by defeating Cervantes on a fifteen-round split-decision, with Ramirez voting for Benitez.

Ramirez employs a number of formal and informal means to stay on top of his game. "I often discuss situations that have occurred or may occur in the ring with fellow referees like Luis Pabon and Joe Cortez," he said. "We discuss how each of us would handle a certain situation. I am in favor of discussing situations that occur or may occur in the ring at referee seminars. Some seminars focus strictly on the rules and regulations, but I prefer to work through situations and have each referee respond on how they would handle a situation instead of just someone providing information that may go in one ear and out the other. As a referee, if I make a mistake in the ring by letting someone take too many punches, it could cost him the boxer's life, or destroy their boxing career. I don't want to live with that."

He'd like to see fight judges get the same scrutiny as referees.

"As referees, we are held accountable for 100 percent of the fights we work, whereas in the 50–60 percent of bouts that end in a knockout, judges are not accountable for their actions," said Ramirez. "In those cases, their scorecards are rarely scrutinized. Even when a fight is stopped early, the judges' scorecards should still be reviewed and discussed for the rounds they scored by the commission and sanctioning organizations. This will help improve the consistency in scoring for judges."

Controversy attached itself to some of Ramirez's own actions in the ring, and he is the first to admit it. A few years ago he refereed a bout in Puerto Rico for the World Boxing Organization's light welterweight title, which aired live on HBO's *Boxing After Dark*. The contestants were Lamont Peterson and France's Willy Blain, both undefeated. In the sixth round of the fight, which Peterson was winning, Blain suddenly grabbed his right arm and starting jumping up and down with a look of pain on his face.

The French boxer didn't understand Spanish or English, and when Ramirez's queries brought no response he stopped the fight. "I thought he broke his hand," he recollected. "When I brought Blain to the ringside doctor, his cornermen were screaming. Then the doctor said there was nothing wrong with Blain's hand and gave his OK for the fight to continue. Based on that, I resumed the bout. When I picked up the cards between rounds, I leaned over and told the commissioner that I had made a mistake by letting the contest continue. Once the referee calls off a contest, it should be over.

"The next round, Blaine started grabbing his right glove again waving it in pain. So I again stopped the fight, this time for good. I really took a verbal beating from the announcers on HBO. Harold Lederman, HBO's 'unofficial official,' gave me the most criticism. Lederman and I go way back; he even had judged fights in which I was the referee. I was surprised he was so critical of me when I re-watched the telecast. But I'll be the first to admit, I did make a mistake that night by letting the fight restart. Fortunately, the right fighter ended up winning the bout."

Ramirez has worked twelve times in Argentina, and always looks forward to going back because he loves the native cuisine and the tango. But refereeing there has not always been a bed of roses for him. On January 15, 1982, Ramirez worked a world super bantamweight title unification bout between native son Sergio Palma and Panamanian Jorge Lujan in front of twenty thousand partisan fans in Cordoba. "During the course of the bout, Palma tried to bite Lujan," recalled Ramirez. "When I saw that, I jumped in and tried to separate the fighters fast and hard. Palma went down on his ass—and the crowd erupted. They thought I had stopped the contest. Twenty thousand angry fans started throwing coins in my direction. I called for time, called over the supervisor and told him that if the crowd didn't stop throwing coins, I would stop the fight and award it to Lujan. An announcement was made and things calmed down and the fight resumed.

"It was back in the days of the fifteen-round title fight, and I also was a judge for the bout and had to score each round. The decision for Palma was unanimous, but the crowd was still upset with me because of what had happened earlier. For safety reasons, the promoter took all the officials to the airport at 2 a.m. to get us out of Argentina as soon as possible."

Another change that has occurred since Ramirez started refereeing is the popularity of female boxing. He once worked a women's world title fight in Panama in which all of a sudden the crowd started yelling and hooting about a situation that even Roberto was unprepared for. The shirt worn by one of the combatants had been rearranged by an uppercut from her opponent, and her breasts flopped out. Ramirez quickly called time and instructed a handler to climb up on the ring apron and hold open a towel while the wardrobe malfunction was corrected.

"Referees have to be prepared for anything, but that was one situation that was never discussed in a seminar!" said Roberto.

Ramirez wants to stay active as a referee as long as physically possible. He is also enthused to mentor his son, Roberto Ramirez Jr. who is now also an international boxing referee. "If I see my son is refereeing a televised bout or if I am in attendance, in my head I am also refereeing the same bout. Fortunately, there have been two occasions in Puerto Rico were Roberto Jr. and I were assigned to referee on the same card."

Roberto is retired from his position as a senior director with the phone company, where he worked primarily in the human resources division for thirty-four years. He also retired after twenty-four years in the National Guard, where he was a lieutenant colonel. But don't expect to see Ramirez retiring from the ring any time soon.

"I have met so many people," Ramirez said, "and I have been able to visit so many wonderful places around the world because of boxing and have never had trouble with anyone. I don't plan on retiring anytime soon."

24

Rafael Ramos

Rafael Ramos is a self-made man who is living the American dream. After growing up in Puerto Rico, Ramos had a successful career in the U.S. Army as well as in boxing. He took advantage of his experiences in both areas to achieve the professional career that he has today, provide him with the guidance in raising his family, and attain his current status as one of the top referees and judges in the sport of boxing. Through his hard work, dedication, and determination, Ramos has had quite a journey.

Mainstream boxing fans will recognize Ramos as the referee for the March 13, 2010, bout between Manny Pacquiao and Joshua Clottey for the WBO welterweight title. The fight, labeled "The Event," took place in front of over forty thousand people in Dallas Cowboys Stadium, Arlington, Texas. He also refereed the 2009 *The Ring* magazine and ESPN Fight of the Year—a back-and-forth war between Juan Manuel Marquez and Juan Diaz for the WBO and WBA lightweight titles.

Few, however, know of his humble and determined beginnings. After graduating from high school in Puerto Rico, Ramos joined the U.S. Army. He spent twenty-one years in military service and was stationed around the world. When he enlisted, he was unable to speak English, but he took the one-time army slogan, "Be All That You Can Be," to heart. Ramos graduated from college, joined the army boxing team, participated in Tae Kwon Do, and learned to be a professional boxing judge and referee, all while giving back to his country.

Ramos competed as a top amateur boxer at 119, 125, and 132 pounds while in the army. He also began practicing martial arts while stationed at Fort Bragg, North Carolina, earning a black belt in Tae Kwon Do in 1986 and winning the North Carolina state silver medal in 1986.

When Ramos could no longer make weight and compete as a boxer, Hank Johnson, the coach of the Fort Bragg boxing team, recruited him to become a referee. He initially resisted, not seeing himself as an official. Johnson, however, insisted and made Ramos come to the gym to work with his fighters.

Johnson had been a boxing mentor for Ramos. The younger brother of former world light heavyweight champion Marvin Johnson, Johnson later became the assistant coach for the successful 1988 U.S. Olympic boxing team. That team, led by Johnson and head coach Kenny Adams, also a career army man (who later became one of boxing's top professional trainers), included four army boxers—Anthony Hembrick and gold medal winners Ray Mercer at heavyweight, Andrew Maynard at light heavyweight, and Kennedy McKinney at bantamweight. With Johnson's influence, Ramos quickly began to officiate, going from bouts at Fort Bragg to the All-Army and United States nationals.

In 1987, Ramos got his license as a judge and started working as a professional boxing official. "My first [professional] fight was for the IBF cruiserweight title, Rickey Parkey and Chisanda Mutti, in Italy," Ramos recalled. "My second professional fight was in December, and was in Korea for an IBF title, which was good, since I was stationed in South Korea at the time.

"In 1988, I applied to become a referee in New Jersey. I was stationed at Fort Dix," Ramos continued. "The commissioner at the time was Larry Hazzard. He made everyone go to shows, watch the referee, watch the judges." In 1989, Ramos received his license. "It was an honor to work in New Jersey. I got to learn from many of the great referees like Frank Cappuccino, Tony Perez, Joe Cortez, and Arthur Mercante Sr."

Later, Ramos would be stationed in Texas. Today, Ramos resides in San Antonio and has been working in the medical field since leaving active duty in 1997. As a clinical research associate, he ensures that physicians comply with Food and Drug Administration (FDA) rules. Ramos reflected on some of the memorable bouts he has refereed, including the aforementioned war between Juan Manuel Marquez and Juan Diaz. It was "one of the greatest fights you will ever see," stated Ramos. "For a minute, I thought Diaz was going to stop Marquez. Marquez was hurt. But Marquez came back to stop him." The 2009 Fight of the Year was ended by a tremendous Marquez right uppercut in the ninth round.

"I also worked another Fight of the Year, Leonard Dorin and Raul Balbi," Ramos remembered, speaking of the January 2002 HBO televised war from San Antonio, Texas, for the WBA lightweight title.

When reflecting on the excitement of the Manny Pacquiao vs. Josh Clottey bout, Ramos said, "There are great memories of the fight. It was a brand new stadium. All of the Cowboys were there, the owner, Mr. Jerry Jones was there. That will forever stay with you.

"If you watch the fight, in the first round, Pacquiao hit Clottey with a left hand in the middle of the chest. Everything changed. Clottey then felt that Pacquiao could stop him. That changed it all—Clottey just covered up. And Pacquiao was not happy. His mission was to KO Clottey," said Ramos of the fight, which was less than a barnburner due to Clottey's reluctance.

That fight was not Ramos's only experience in huge sports stadiums. "I also worked the Mike Jones vs. Jesus Soto Karass fight on the [Manny] Pacquiao vs. Antonio Margarito undercard," said Ramos, speaking of the November 2010 war at Cowboy Stadium. "I also worked the undercard of Julio Cesar Chavez vs. Pernell Whitaker," he said, referring to the September 10, 1993, bout at San Antonio's Alamodome, featuring boxing's top two pound-for-pound fighters of the day.

"You talk about fights that stick in your memory. One fight is the comeback of Evander Holyfield," recalled Ramos, of the August 18, 2006, victory of then forty-four-year-old former heavyweight champion Evander Holyfield over Jeremy Bates at the American Airlines Center in Dallas, Texas. "Holyfield is a superstar. I had seen him on TV, but never in person. It was an honor to work that fight. Anything could happen. It could have been Holyfield's last fight if he lost. If he won, he could get going [to the top again]. In the second round, Bates was talking a lot of punishment, and I stopped it. And to me it was an excellent stoppage. Bates was going to get hurt, because Holyfield has no mercy [in the ring].

"I also refereed the first professional world title fight in Ecuador," said Ramos of the December 1994, Frankie Liles vs. Michael Nunn fight on the Bernard Hopkins vs. Segundo Mercado card in Quito, Ecuador. "It was an honor, and I got to meet 'the Greatest' Muhammad Ali."

Boxing has brought Ramos all over Europe, the Far East, and Latin America. With his background in martial arts, he has also refereed some Mixed Martial Arts matches. He has also refereed the Wilfredo Vasquez Sr. vs. Orlando Canizales bout. He was the third man in the ring for bouts involving Michael Carbajal, Devon Alexander, Jorge Arce, Brandon Rios, Victor Ortiz, Julio Cesar Chavez Jr., Edwin Valero, Abner Mares, Fernando Montiel, Tony Ayala Jr., Jesse James Lejia, Paulie Ayala, Gabriel Ruelas, Hector Camacho, Kennedy McKinney, and Junior Jones.

"On December 31, 2011, I judged a WBA title fight in Japan, and [that night] I also refereed a WBA world title fight. Japan has the nicest people. They treat you very well," said Ramos, who has visited the country twenty-three times. "I have a special place in my heart for Japan because I refereed a fight on May 19, 2008, between Yusuke Kubori and Jose Alfaro. The day I left to Japan, my mother, Rosa, passed away [after he had left]. I was informed upon my arrival. I knew I would not make it back in time for the funeral, so being a professional I stayed to do the fight. The people from Japan showed me tremendous support in my time of need—the Japan Boxing Commission honored my mother and my family with the ten-bell count."

"In Korea, people remember me when I return for fights," recalled Ramos. "I used to train Korean fighters when I was stationed over there."

Ramos once officiated a fight in a city in Thailand across the river from Laos. "We flew in to Bangkok, and had to fly to another town," he recalled. "We were in Thailand, but you could see Laos across the river. It was most impressive. And [there was] this man at the fights, he was like the 'king of the city.' And he was sitting on a throne during the whole fight. And I kept looking at him, and he kept looking at me. I kept looking at that river, and told myself, 'If you make a mistake, they are going to throw you in the river!'"

Ramos advised aspiring officials with a goal of becoming a boxing referee, "You have to know the rules and regulations. That is most important. If you don't know, don't go inside the ring.

"Second, you have to have experience as an amateur referee. Anyone can get in the ring and be a referee, but when things get tough, you have to make decisions. That is what separates a good from a bad referee," added Ramos. "You don't have to be an ex-boxer. Just because you are an ex-boxer does not mean you will be a good referee. But a referee has to be able to anticipate what will happen. Whether a fighter will throw a left, or throw a right. The way fighters move. And you can only know that if you were a fighter or spend a lot of time working at the local gym, with fighters. That's how you become better.

"Boxing is a brutal sport," Ramos warned young people who want to become boxers. "There are trainers, and coaches and they think they know how to train, but they don't. You have to know the basics. You have to know how to move. You have to know how to jab. And not a lot of people know how to do that today. Those traits are gone. The first thing is to learn the basics of boxing."

Ramos is intensely proud of his family. He has been married to his wife, Elena, since 1977, and they have two children—a son, Alexis, and a daughter, Marelyn. His daughter has a master's degree in human resources and has been involved in the Wounded Warrior Project, which assists severely injured servicemen in their transition from active duty to civilian life. She worked as a case manager assistant for the program, before leaving to obtain her master's. "I love my family. I always push my children to be better than me," he said.

"When I got out of high school, it was tough. Being from Puerto Rico, [I was] a United States citizen. Going into the Army was a different culture. Learning English was very tough. But I had married. I knew I had to take care of my family. I knew it was a way to serve my country," remembered Ramos.

Alexis is a member of the U.S. Army, like his father. Also, like his father, he became a boxer and has fought for ten years. He won regional titles in

Texas in 2001 before joining the army in 2006. A public affairs specialist, Alexis won All-Army titles at 125 pounds in 2007, 2009, and 2010, as well as All-Armed Forces titles in those same years. He participated in the 2008 U.S. Olympic trials. Only eight fighters in each weight division earn that honor.

Perhaps no one is more fit than Alexis Ramos to comment on the character and abilities of his father. "As a father . . . he is an exceptional father figure, and a role model. Look at his military career. When he started, he did not speak any English. And he did twenty-one years in the army. He got his bachelor's degree. And the type of jobs he has had since then tells you about him. No amount of words can tell you my respect for him, my gratitude for him . . . There are no words to tell you what type of father he has been. He has influenced me into going into boxing. He has influenced me going into the army. But he did not want me to fight. He especially did not want me to fight at a young age . . . I know he did not want me to sustain trauma to the head," said Alexis in an interview with the authors. "My father is a great father. And he is the best referee in boxing."

25

Jack Reiss

Growing up in Brooklyn, Jack Reiss and his brother were introduced to boxing by their father in an unconventional way. Instead of outfitting them with regular boxing gloves, he had the boys put several layers of socks on each hand when they sparred. They lost their dad when Jack was eight, but their father's interest in boxing stayed with them.

As a youngster, Reiss competed in amateur smokers around Brooklyn and avidly followed the sport. "As a kid, me and my friends never had any money, so when the closed-circuit telecasts for the big fights like Ali vs. Frazier were aired at local theaters, we had to get creative to get everyone into the theater," he said. "We passed a hat, each kid threw in two bucks, and one kid would buy a ticket and after he entered the theater he would run to the back door, where the rest of us hid outside, and let us all in to watch the fight."

But it was actually hockey at which Reiss excelled at a young age. By the time he was sixteen he played on several traveling teams. "I wasn't the main scorer, but I did get into my share of scraps on the ice and I took over the role of enforcer," he said. "Some kids attended hockey camp to improve on their game; I headed to a nearby karate school to improve my skills."

Reiss's success on the ice led to an invitation to try out with the Welland Sabres, the Buffalo Sabres farm team. But Reiss passed on that and turned his attention to boxing and kickboxing instead. In a kickboxing match against an opponent who outweighed him by fifty-three pounds, Reiss broke his right foot when a roundhouse kick connected with the other guy's elbow. "I was twenty-three years old at the time, and I headed out to California to recuperate from the injury," he recalled. "But once I got to California, I never left."

Reiss then began a career as a firefighter in Los Angeles. He spent his spare time attending as many professional boxing matches and Los Angeles Kings hockey games as possible, until his wife, Josephine, told him that he should devote more time to her and their sons, Joseph and Riley.

Not wanting to give up his two favorite pastimes, Reiss sat down and tried to figure out a way to turn his passions into a job. "So I called the Los Angeles Kings to see if they were looking to hire anyone and had no luck," he said. "At the time, most of the major fights were happening in Las Vegas, so I also reached out to Mark Ratner of the Nevada State Athletic Commission. He advised me to give the California State Athletic Commission a call to see how to get licensed to be a professional boxing referee there."

The timing was perfect. The Golden State boxing commission was inaugurating a brand new program for apprentice boxing officials. "I was accepted into a class of ninety-two people that had applied to be either a judge or referee," said Reiss. "The whole process took three years. We met approximately every three weeks and went over situations that pertained to refereeing and judging professional boxing matches and had tests following each session. Referees Pat Russell, Larry Rozadilla, Lou Filippo, and Marty Denkin taught the course and did a tremendous job.

"Out of the ninety-two that started out in the course, only a handful made it to become judges and referees. On the final day, we had to take a one-hour exam and decide if we wanted to be a referee, a judge, or both. I passed the exam to become both a certified professional boxing judge and referee."

To prepare for his new vocation, Reiss went to different boxing gyms around LA and got into the ring with boxers for their sparring sessions. "I showed up at the LA Boxing Club where Sugar Shane Mosley and Genaro

Hernandez trained, and got in the ring when they sparred," he said. "I was a fire marshal at the time for the LAFD, used my flex-hours to go to the gyms in early afternoons. Working with these champions provided a real education that paid off for me early in my career as a referee.

"For my first assignment," recalled Reiss, "I worked one four-round fight on a boxing card under the supervision of one of the state's experienced referees who was assigned to be my mentor for the evening. He and the other mentors paid fifty dollars out of their own purses for our pay for the night. This went on for several months. I worked one fight a month and would get critiqued at the end of the night. It was a great learning experience. Referees like Marty Denkin and Pat Russell were patient with us and were very giving of their knowledge. Eventually, I started working six- and eight-round bouts, and then graduated to main events."

Reiss's refereeing career has taken him to Mexico many times. The fans there are very passionate and don't hesitate to let the referee know when they disagree with his decision. Sometimes they do it in very novel ways.

"Once I worked a bout between two Mexican boxers and stopped the action to examine a cut suffered by one of them," recalled Reiss. "The crowd thought I was stopping the fight, and all of a sudden all kinds of debris was being tossed into the ring. I ducked away from a white flying object that missed me by inches and exploded when it hit the canvas. It was a loaded diaper! Then a full plastic bottle of Gatorade drilled me right in the head."

A referee needs to keep his focus at all times while in the ring. This rule applies even at Hugh Hefner's Playboy Mansion, where Reiss has refereed a few times in recent years. "It's a legendary place where everybody is brought in by limo and there are celebrities and beautiful woman everywhere," he said. "ESPN has broadcast some shows I have refereed in the mansion's backyard. It's fun seeing all the celebrities, and you can always count on seeing Hugh Hefner with plenty of attractive women around him."

Reiss has become something of a celebrity himself since becoming a top-flight referee. In the movie *Ali*, starring Will Smith, Reiss was cast as legendary referee Arthur Mercante for the film's depiction of the first battle between Muhammad Ali and Joe Frazier. In the opening scene of the Ben Affleck movie *Daredevil*, Reiss was shown refereeing a fight. He also had a role in Mark Wahlberg's film, *The Fighter*, but his scenes ended up on the cutting room floor.

"Mark Wahlberg was a great guy to meet," said Reiss, "and although my scene didn't make it in the movie I still got paid!"

In 2005, Sylvester Stallone, Sugar Ray Leonard, and television producer Mark Burnett dreamed up a boxing reality show called *The Contender*. The show featured real professional boxers competing in a tournament, with all bouts sanctioned by the California State Athletic Commission. The commission picked the referees for the show, and one of them was Reiss.

Stallone and his brother Frank were often on the set during filming. "Both Sylvester and Frank Stallone were great guys," said Reiss. "They were true boxing fans and they gravitated to the referees because they knew we were also boxing people. As the series progressed, Sylvester and Frank and the producers formed a good bond with the referees and the state athletic commission, and they would come to us looking for an explanation of something that occurred in or out of the ring and seek our opinion on how to deal with it. I was a fire marshal in real life, and at times also felt like one on the set," quipped Reiss about having to put out the "fires" that occurred on the set.

"Also, I was an inspector for the State of California, and I would be sent to evaluate boxers sparring at various gyms throughout the state [making sure they were fit to fight]," recalled Reiss. "I sometimes took fighters to Freddie Roach's Wild Card Gym for the evaluation. It was close to my fire station. While there, I often saw Frank Stallone training. He knew his stuff."

Reiss was involved in all four seasons of *The Contender*. The last one was filmed in Singapore, where producer Mark Burnett had done some previous filming on different projects with good results. Burnett intended to use local boxing referees and judges throughout the four-week series shoot, but that didn't pan out. The officials originally selected for *The Contender IV* had backgrounds in Muay Thai, an Oriental martial art that has some similarities to boxing but has a wholly different scoring system.

Early on a Sunday morning, Reiss received a call at his fire station. It was from Singapore, and the message was simple: HELP!

"When I asked what I could do," recalled Reiss, "they said, 'How about getting on the next plane to Singapore? And could you bring another referee with you?' Within twenty-four hours, Pat Russell and I were on a plane to Singapore.

"It was one of the cleanest places I had ever been. The people there treated us very well. Pat and I conducted seminars for the judges the day we arrived and we both split the refereeing duties for all of the remaining bouts."

Reiss keeps busy conducting seminars for referees and judges in boxing. One of the seminars, "The Theory of Stopping Fights—A Scientific Approach," is based on his years of experience assessing trauma victims as a firefighter, emergency medical technician, and professional referee. As a firefighter and paramedic, when Reiss is called to an accident scene where a victim has incurred head trauma, he tries to piece together what happened. It's the same when it comes to gauging the condition of a boxer.

"When I am assessing trauma I like to get a baseline," he stated. "As a referee I try to look at what is normal, I watch films of the fighters to get an idea of where they are physically when a fight starts so I will be able to pick up any signs of deterioration during the fight. When a fighter gets knocked down in the first round, and there has been little history of trauma for the bout I will usually let the fight continue, but if the same knockdown occurred in a later round I might stop the fight based on the amount of damage that has been inflicted throughout the contest.

"I assess if a fighter has taken enough punishment based on his body language. I try to look for signs that show me the fighter is not as alert as he was when first entering the ring. After a knockdown I may ask him to walk to me, or I may ask them to hold out one of their gloved hands to me. In the dressing room before the fight, I tell all the boxers, 'I will not allow you to take a beating in my ring and don't care who gets mad at me if I stop a fight.' I sometimes need to protect a fighter from himself and his corner. I don't want a fighter to get hurt beyond what he needs to in the course of determining a winner in the bout."

Reiss watches replays of the bouts he works to gauge his performance and learn from any mistakes. He also relies on colleagues to assess his performance and give him feedback from their professional perspective.

"After each bout, I'll discuss my performance with colleagues like Marty Denkin or Pat Russell, and sometimes even referees from other states, like Kenny Bayless, Benjy Esteves, and Elmo Adolph (who passed away on August 9, 2012, after this interview was conducted). If it's an MMA fight I'll consult with MMA referee 'Big' John McCarthy," Reiss explained. "We try to be as objective with each other as possible; it's not about flattery. I'm fortunate to have this type of close support that continually allows me to learn and improve as a referee. We bounce plenty of suggestions off each other and learn from each other.

"Big John McCarthy and I have been working together a lot in recent times. We review a lot of boxing and MMA fights together and pick them apart. John was recently certified to referee boxing matches in California, and I've been a MMA referee and judge for years. In fact, I took a course on MMA officiating from John. A relatively new wrinkle in California is hybrid cards consisting of both boxing and MMA fights. At a recent one consisting of four boxing matches and seven MMA bouts, I refereed the MMA portion and Big John refereed the boxing end of it." Whether it's boxing or MMA, Reiss is constantly learning. Take the match he refereed in 2005 between "Mighty" Mike Arnaoutis and Roberto Santa Cruz, for example. The undefeated Arnaoutis was an aggressive fighter and he took control at the opening bell. "After watching Cruz backpedal and take some heavy shots in the first three rounds, I thought about stopping the fight," recalled Reiss. "To me it was a one-sided affair, and after the third round I went over to Cruz's corner and said to his trainer, Rudy Hernandez, 'You have got to show me something soon or I'll have to stop the fight.'

"Rudy stood up and said calmly, 'Jack, relax; it's a twelve round fight, and twelve rounds is a long time.' Cruz picked up the tempo after that, and after twelve rounds he lost a disputed majority decision. That taught me to be careful about what I anticipate in the ring. It was actually Cruz's strategy to be on defense-mode in the opening rounds and then get more aggressive as the fight progressed. And he almost pulled off an upset. As a referee, it taught me to be careful about injecting myself too much into a fight."

Each year there is a charity boxing event pitting a team of amateur boxers from the LAFD against a team made up of Los Angeles police officers and sheriff's deputies. In 1986, Reiss competed in the 160-pound division and took home a gold medal. Since then he has trained boxers for the event and helped with matchmaking and refereeing.

California has more boxing shows than any other state in the nation, and Reiss doesn't lack for opportunities to practice and perfect his craft. He's often approached by fans who watched him referee a big televised match and liked what they saw. He gets a kick out of that, and an even bigger kick out of telling them, "It only took me fourteen years to become an overnight sensation!"

26

Celestino Ruiz

Boxing has always been a sport that tough young men from difficult economic situations would try their hands at, in hopes of making something of themselves. Youngsters dream of riches, the type earned by Oscar De La Hoya and Floyd Mayweather. A very select few make that amount of money. Countless others learn life's lessons as boys and teenagers, and become outstanding men. Chicago referee Celestino Ruiz, from the hard, gang-infested streets of the Humboldt Park neighborhood, is an illustration of a boxing success story. He is widely regarded as one of the top young up-and-coming referees in boxing. He gives credit to the sport for helping make him the man he is, and he is not hesitant to give back to the sport, acting as one of its outstanding ambassadors.

Ruiz has been refereeing as a professional since 2007, and quickly began working in important fights. The first professional fight he refereed was on October 13, 2007, at the Sears Center in Hoffman Estates, Illinois, and involved future IBF and WBC light welterweight champion Devon Alexander. The bout was part of the undercard of an HBO televised IBF, WBA, and WBO lightweight title unification match, with Juan Diaz stopping Julio Diaz in nine. Months earlier, Ruiz had judged his first professional boxing match, while working the Julio Cesar Chavez Jr. vs. Louis Brown bout. The August 4, 2007, match was part of an HBO pay-per-view televised card, with David Diaz and Erik Morales in the main event.

Ruiz brings a near-lifetime of experience into the ring. He began boxing at the age of nine. He had more than one hundred amateur fights, and won a Catholic Youth Organization title. His extensive amateur career saw him fight around the country. He had approximately eighty fights and several wins over future two-time world title challenger Lorenzo Smith. Ruiz also fought 1996 Olympic alternate Darnell Wilson three times, beating him once. Kenny Gould, the 1992 Olympian from Rockford, Illinois, was another of Ruiz's amateur opponents.

Ruiz spent seven years as an amateur official before making the move to the professional ranks. He judged for two years, and then refereed for five years. He feels it was a positive experience to have amateur and professional judging experience, so he knows how the judge feels and also knows the importance of staying out of the way so they can observe the action. Ruiz indicated that it is very important for a referee to keep moving throughout a bout and to know where his judges are. He tries never to block a judge's line of sight. Ruiz maintains a breakneck boxing schedule, working several amateur shows a month in the Chicago area as well as the twelve-night Chicago Golden Gloves tournament. "I will always work amateur shows. I love boxing. Working amateur shows keeps me sharp. It also lets me see the up-and-coming fighters in Chicago, see who is going to be the next group of pros. That way I will know how they fight, know how they move."

Every Saturday, as well as at least two times during the week, Ruiz can be found in the boxing ring at local gyms. "I am in the gym, working sparring, jumping rope, hitting the bags," he said. "The minute I see people sparring, I jump into the ring. I love moving around, staying used to being in there. It helps them out. It helps me out as well."

Ruiz has worked for the Chicago Transit Authority (CTA) repairing trains since 1992. He has often balanced odd shifts with his work in boxing.

"Boxing straightened me out," Ruiz explained of boxing's influence on his life. "It was my way out of a lot of trouble. I grew up in a neighborhood where there is an influence of gangs. But when you got to get up, run, train, and think, *who am I going to fight next*, it keeps you out of trouble. When I didn't focus, that is when I got in problems. When I did focus 100 percent, there were no problems. I can relate to some of these young guys that are fighting at a young age. Then they get to high school, and they lose interest in the game. It takes lots of training and focus. These guys think they are missing out—missing out on girls and messing around. When you have lost focus, when I lost focus—that's when you have problems. Boxing did me a lot of good. If it wasn't for boxing, I wouldn't be around."

Ruiz himself had dropped out of Roberto Clemente High School for two years before returning, graduating, and later going to work for the CTA. Ruiz is driven by an intense desire to learn more about officiating and how to prepare for every possibility. He has gone to Las Vegas and worked with veteran referee Joe Cortez at his home gym.

After deducting points from a fighter in a recent contest, Ruiz spent time going over his decision with high-level officials and commissioners to make sure he had made the right call. He contacted Missouri's Tim Lueckenhoff, the executive director in the Office of Athletics and president of the Association of Boxing Commissions (ABC). He also discussed the deduction with legendary Nevada judge Duane Ford, who often gives ABC officials training around the country, as well as some local officials.

His quest for knowledge and running through all possible scenarios paid off in a contest he worked in Puerto Rico, in October 2011. He was officiating a four-round bout between two newcomers, Jesus Pagan and Israel Vasquez (brother of world champion Wilfredo Vasquez Jr. and son of former champion Wilfredo Vasquez Sr.), at the close of the WBO Convention. In the first round, both fighters threw punches. Both fighters landed punches. Both fighters were put on the canvas—a rare double knockdown. Ruiz immediately picked up the count from the timekeeper and counted. When the first fighter, Vasquez, got up he began to celebrate as his opponent was still down. Ruiz immediately directed Vasquez to a neutral corner, which suspended the count. Ruiz then resumed the count until Pagan got up. His preparedness readied him for the situation. "One time I talked to Joe Cortez, we were going through scenarios, and that was the first one he brought up," recalled Ruiz of the double knockdown. "I knew what to do in that situation."

Ruiz has worked fights with multiple-time world champs Jhonny Gonzalez and Cory Spinks. He refereed a regional title between Ghana's Osumanu Adama and former world-title challenger Angel Hernandez. He has been the third man in bouts featuring contenders and former Olympians Deontay Wilder, Gary Russell Jr., and Ireland's Andy Lee. He has also refereed bouts with prospects Donovan George and Shawn Porter.

Ruiz has a commanding presence in the ring. Like many top third men, he believes that establishing command begins by taking control in the locker room. "It is very important to take control of a fight inside a dressing room. You should take control of the whole locker room. If a fighter is sitting there with headphones on, I tell him to take them off. If people are playing the radio or music loudly, I make them turn down the radio," related Ruiz.

"Sometimes the locker room is busy, crowded, with lots of activity. I will say 'guys, slow down.' I will make the fighter and his chief second sit in a seat. I will tell them I am going to go through everything now, because I don't want to be explaining to them later in the locker room why I stopped the fight. I go through the rules, such as no standing eight count and that I will stop it if they take excessive blows. I let them know, if they show me a way out, they are going to get a way out. And that is by not throwing punches. If you don't throw punches, and you are taking punches, I am going to stop the fight. You have to fight back. I let them know my job is to protect them. That's why I'm here."

In a recent bout in Indiana, Ruiz gave his pre-fight instructions to a fighter and his cornerman in the locker room. The fighter told Ruiz, with bravado, "All I'm letting you know, is if that motherfucker hits me low, I'm gonna hit him low," and then launched into a slew of expletives. Ruiz quickly took control and told the boxer, warning, "Now that you told me, and now that I've heard that, I'm giving you a warning. If you commit a foul, and throw a low blow, I am going to take a point off."

"I did not want him to feel he could get into the ring and do what he wanted to do," Ruiz explained. Perhaps predictably, the fighter went down three times in the first round, and the fight was stopped. "As macho as this guy was in the locker room, he didn't even really get hit hard, and he went down. Once the fight started, this guy just wanted to get his money, get paid, and leave."

Ruiz sees his role as protecting the fighter, sometimes from himself. Ruiz was the third man in a February 2008 contest between Chicago prospect Francisco Rodriguez and lesser-known visitor Andre Wilson. The bout was nationally televised on Spanish language Telefutura network show *Solo Boxeo*. Rodriguez had won the Chicago Golden Gloves five times from 2000 to 2004, as well as a national title in 2001. In the second round, Wilson badly floored Rodriguez twice. Rodriguez got up, but Ruiz saw that "his eyes were jumpy, and it was clear he had a concussion," so he waved off the bout. Rodriguez's trainers and family criticized Ruiz for stopping the fight too early. Several relatives of Rodriguez even swore at Ruiz when he came down to the dressing room later to give another fighter pre-fight instructions. The family filed a formal complaint with the boxing commission for an unjust and premature stoppage. The complaint did not go anywhere, and the stoppage was upheld.

On November 20, 2009, Rodriguez challenged undefeated Teon Kennedy for the United States Boxing Association (USBA) title at the Blue Horizon in Philadelphia. Rodriguez took punishment throughout the match, and the fight was stopped in the tenth round. He later slipped into a coma and died. Rodriguez's organs were donated, saving the lives of the five people who were able to receive transplants. The story of the fatal bout and the subsequent organ donation was chronicled on the ESPN televised sports newsmagazine *E:60*, in the story "Hero."

"I think Francisco Rodriguez was a fighter with a lot of balls, a lot of heart. Maybe too much heart," opined Ruiz. "Every fight of his was a war. Even his sparring sessions were wars. He was a guy willing to die in the ring. Sometimes guys like that need to be protected from themselves." Ruiz also reflected on the desire and tenacity of those who become boxers, stating, "About 85 percent of these boxers, they are not going to quit unless you do it for them. This isn't MMA, these guys don't tap out."

Ruiz is quick to thank many of those who have helped put him in the position he is in today. "I am thankful for Mauro DiFiore, one of my former boxing coaches," he said of the veteran boxing judge from Chicago who coached him as a youth. "I thank Al Ortiz Sr., he helped me a lot. He was one of my coaches. He is a retired Chicago fireman." Ruiz is also grateful for veteran Chicago trainer George Hernandez, a coach at Garfield Park boxing gym, in Chicago. Hernandez has coached numerous local professionals, including 2000 Olympic heavyweight Michael Bennett. Ruiz is a regular at Garfield Park; honing his skills as a third man working sparring matches. Ruiz also thanks Sam Colonna, who is considered to be the most accomplished of all Chicago boxing trainers and who has worked with a long list of contenders. "When I was boxing, he was the coach at the Valentine Boys Club, and they were one of the only clubs that would accept anyone, give you an opportunity to come in and work," Ruiz explained. "When I started to want to learn how to referee, Sam had the Windy City Gym and he told me, 'Come into my gym anytime, practice.' And I would always go in there and work sparring matches."

Ruiz indicates that a future goal of his is to operate a boxing gym for at-risk kids. "I'd like to work in a gym, in the inner city, and teach these kids how to box, and some discipline," he said. "I can tell these kids, 'Boxing can help you. It helped me.' If you eat and sleep boxing, you won't be thinking about the streets." Ruiz's quick rise up the ranks of professional boxing referees can be attributed to his determination, desire, and his quest for knowledge. Fighting once gave Ruiz his drive. Today, he experiences a new type of desire—to continue to improve as a referee and as a top-level official. "Competition was always good for me. It gave me hunger. But today, I am still hungry. It's a new type of hunger."

27

Pat Russell

"I have tremendous respect for fighters. I respect the incredible violence. Things can turn, and turn quickly. It is taking a kid out into deep water, and you don't want him to drown," said Pat Russell, sharing a philosophical moment. "I have nothing but respect for athletes. There is no such thing as a cowardly fighter. I never met one. It takes so much guts—to expose what you can, and even more, what you can't do. You are out there with a guy trying to knock your block off."

Russell, a referee, judge, and member of the California Boxing Hall of Fame, has had a life worthy of tremendous respect. He has demonstrated bravery and compassion, distinguishing himself in and outside the sport of boxing.

A Vietnam veteran, Russell served as a member of the U.S. Army from 1970 to 1974, including a one-year stint as an infantry platoon leader from 1971 to 1972. He continued his service in the Reserves, from 1977 to 1998, where he qualified as a member of the Special Forces and retired as a captain. Russell's commitment to public service continued after his active duty was completed, as he worked in law enforcement for thirty-one years, the majority of them with the San Diego County State's Attorney's Office as an investigator.

Russell never saw himself as becoming a boxing referee. He boxed as a youngster, and had hoped to compete in the 1980 California Police

Olympics, but an old war injury prevented him from doing so. In 1981, he began refereeing. This led from the amateur ranks into professional ranks, and eventually to the top of the sport.

Russell remains active in the United States Police and Fire Games, serving as a director and chief boxing official. "The qualities that people in law enforcement possess, that military or firefighters have, make for a good referee or judge. You need to make instant decisions, and live with them," reflected Russell. "Police and military, they operate on instinct. They are trained to act. It is like a boxer. A boxer throws the left hook. He didn't think, 'I'm going to throw a left hook.' He sees the opening, and reacts."

Russell is quick to credit the great mentors he had in the sport, and admits that he is always learning. "When I started, there was a great referee and judge, Dick Young," said Russell of the man who was a top official from the early 1940s until shortly before his death in 2001. "Dick told me, 'Always count out a champ.' He meant that to these fighters, fighting for a title means so much. We officials owe it to them to be at our very best."

Russell's first title fight was for the North American Boxing Federation junior flyweight title on August 17, 1989. "Tony 'Bazooka' DeLuca, from San Diego, was fighting. He was a popular local guy. He drew crowds to the old El Cortez Hotel," recalled Russell. "He was fighting a real tough guy from Mexico, a veteran, Willy Salazar. In the eighth round, DeLuca was winning, and he just got hit with a shot, and went out.

"I started counting, and was thinking of Young's words, 'always count out a champ, kid.' And then DeLuca just woke up, at like three or four. And he got up! And I couldn't believe it. I asked him, 'Are you OK?' And he said, 'Yes, could you please get out of my way!' And then he won the fight. I see DeLuca now, we are friends. He is a cancer survivor, and we always laugh together about that fight and that moment."

Russell is not an advocate of referees judging the fight, since he prefers to concentrate on only the safety of the fighter, not scoring a bout at the same time. Yet he is also one of the world's top judges. Early on in his career, Russell judged a fight where he scored a very close round "10–10"—meaning that he had it as an even round.

"I was a younger official, and was very happy with my score of 10–10. It was a very close round," said Russell. "Dick Young called me out on it, and said, 'so after the seventy-five miles of roadwork these guys did, the forty-five rounds of sparring, and the hours of work they put in the gym, you sat there for three solid minutes, and couldn't make a decision?' It was an interesting perspective. And it propelled me to be a better judge. I think I have had about three even rounds in my entire judging career."

Young also advised Russell early on that "no one comes to see you dance," letting him know that it was not him, but the fighters, that were the stars of the show. Russell also credits California-based officials such as John Thomas, Chuck Haslett, Larry Rozadilla, and Lou Filippo with assisting and advising him and taking him under their wings. "They would critique me and they were great mentors."

Russell has worked some of boxing's biggest bouts as both a judge and a referee. He has been the third man in such contests as Timothy Bradley vs. Lamont Peterson, Shane Mosley vs. Sergio Mora, Bernard Hopkins vs. Chad Dawson, Israel Vazquez vs. Rafael Marquez III, Antonio Tarver vs. Glen Johnson I, Bernard Hopkins vs. Glen Johnson, James Toney vs. Tim Littles, and Brian Mitchell vs. Tony Lopez. He has also refereed bouts involving Sergio Martinez, Andre Ward, Vernon Forrest, Riddick Bowe, Terry Norris, Michael Moorer, Edwin Valero, Joel Casamayor, Juan Manuel Marquez, Michael Carbajal, Mark "Too Sharp" Johnson, Humberto Gonzalez, Oscar De La Hoya, and Johnny Tapia.

Pat Russell has sat ringside as a judge for major fights such as Lennox Lewis vs. Vitali Klitschko, Shane Mosley vs. Oscar De La Hoya I, Vic Darchinyan vs. Jorge Arce, Shane Mosley vs. Ricardo Mayorga, Ricky Hatton vs. Juan Lazcano, Rafael Marquez vs. Israel Vazquez I, Chris Byrd vs. DaVarryl Williamson, Leonard Dorin vs. Paul Spadafora, and Rafael Ruelas vs. Freddie Pendleton. He has also judged matches featuring Jermain Taylor, Orlando Salido, Brian Viloria, Ronald "Winky" Wright, and Humberto Gonzalez.

Russell also appeared in the movie *Ali* as a referee, and worked as a referee in the televised boxing reality show *The Contender*.

When asked about his most memorable matches, Russell chose the Marquez vs. Vazquez fights—the four classic wars between world champions

Israel Vazquez and Rafael Marquez, brother of Juan Manuel Marquez, fought between 2007 and 2010. The fighters split the four contests, with Marquez winning the first fight and the final fight, and Vazquez taking the middle two.

Russell judged the first fight and refereed the third, which was the 2008 ESPN and *The Ring* magazine fight of the year. The second fight, which Russell did not work, was the ESPN and *The Ring* magazine 2007 fight of the year. "Those were ferocious fights. The third one was incredible. I respect all fighters, but those guys really deserve respect. Marco Antonio Barrera and Kennedy McKinney was also a great fight," said Russell of the first Main Event on HBO's *Boxing After Dark*. "Shane Mosley and Oscar De La Hoya was also a great one. Such incredibly quick hands. And [future hall of famer] Terry Norris as well," reflected Russell on some of the other memorable fighters and fights he officiated in.

The Lennox Lewis vs. Vitali Klitschko fight was a heavyweight war, and it was the last of Lewis's great career. Russell was a judge for the June 21, 2003, match at the Staples Center in Los Angeles. Fighting was stopped by the doctor after six rounds due to a huge cut over Klitschko's left eye, which a Lewis right hand had caused in the third round. Lewis won by a technical knockout, but at the time of the stoppage, Russell and the two other judges had Klitschko winning 58–56, or four rounds for Klitschko and two for Lewis.

Russell said that the duties and the importance of the referee are tremendous. They have to live with the decisions they make—sometimes life and death decisions. "I believe Joyce Carol Oates said, 'the referee is the conscience of the audience.'

"I care about all officials. Several top referees have committed suicide," added Russell, referring to top Nevada referees Richard Green, Toby Gibson, and Mitch Halpern. Green and Halpern had both been referees in boxing contests where a participant died. "An official should be concerned with the safety of the fighters, and want a fair and even fight. It should not be to get their face on television, and to self-promote," said Russell, adding that he critiques and accepts criticism of his work to this day, for the betterment of himself and his work. His philosophy is that the "most important fight is his next fight. Whether it is a four-round fight, or a championship fight."

28

Gerald Scott

Years ago Gerald Scott looked at his wife, Brenda, and wondered, "What could I do to travel and see the world—and get paid for it?" Then the answer dawned on him: "I'll get back into boxing and become a referee!"

Since then boxing has taken Scott to Mexico, Germany, and England, among other foreign locales. But Chicago is where he sees most of his action, having worked most of the major cards in the area for the last decade.

The Windy City fight scene has a steady fan base, and usually local announcers use the prefix "gentleman" when introducing referee Gerald Scott to the crowd. The appellation is often misused, but not in this case. Those familiar with the mild-mannered referee rarely see anything but a friendly side of Scott, and vice-versa. "I haven't met anybody I didn't like in the fight game," he says. "It's amazing for my involvement in such a violent sport to have met so many wonderful people."

But as a youth battling race issues at a predominantly white Catholic high school on Chicago's south side, Scott sometimes had to act less than gentlemanly, and occasionally duked it out with his antagonists right in the classroom.

Scott developed a passion for boxing at an early age. He recalls watching televised fights with his father in the 1950s and '60s, featuring such

169

staples of the game as Rubin "Hurricane" Carter, Carl "Bobo" Olson, and Jimmy Dupree. "As a kid," he remembered, "I used to save up my spare change and then spend hours at a dime arcade located near the burlesque theater in Chicago. I used to watch boxing reels of guys like Sugar Ray Robinson and Willie Pep. A dime would only get you a portion of a fight and I used to spend three or four hours at a time watching the fights at the arcade. I always looked up to Sugar Ray Robinson."

A makeshift boxing gym, located a few doors down from his residence, was where he and other neighborhood kids trained daily and learned the fundamentals of the sport. What he learned then helped Scott in impromptu fights in high school. "There were times racial insults led to fisticuffs," he said. "If someone insulted me or a friend, I told them we would settle it immediately after class. The offending classmate along with onlooking students would find an empty classroom and fists would fly. After the fight was over we shook hands and no one would inform the administration of the scuffles. I had more than one of these altercations."

An early boxing mentor for Scott was Chuck Bodak, the legendary cut-man who later worked the corners of Muhammad Ali, Oscar De La Hoya, and numerous other world champions. Bodak trained Scott at the Catholic Youth Organization gym in Chicago. In 1969, Bodak was with Rocky Marciano on the night before the former undefeated heavyweight champion was killed in a plane crash. In fact, the last photograph Marciano ever took was with Bodak.

"Chuck was one of the first people to teach me the fundamentals of boxing," stated Scott. "He often spoke of his relationship with Rocky Marciano. I am glad he went on to so much success in the sport as a cornerman. His passion for the sport eventually became my passion as well."

It didn't take long. Scott recalls that when the Washington Redskins came to Chicago to play the Bears in 1963, President John F. Kennedy was going to be at the game. Scott also had an opportunity to see the game, but "I chose to go to the gym instead to train. I did whatever I could to improve as a boxer."

A year later, he tacked a few years on to his age so that he could enter the Chicago Golden Gloves tournament held at St. Rita's Catholic High

School. "I went out and gave it my best shot," he recalled. "The referee stopped my fight in the second round. I was a little disappointed but I didn't question the referee. And even though [my boxing career] didn't last long, it has helped me as a referee to have competed as a boxer." When Scott decided to become a boxing referee some years later, he started going to a park district gym. "I didn't know anybody there," he said, "but I just got inside the ring and started moving around. I would also referee as many sparring sessions as possible."

After several months of that, he registered to get certified as a referee in the amateur ranks. Chicago-based referee Genaro "Gino" Rodriguez conducted Scott's initial official's certification clinic and would become one of his key mentors. "At the completion of the clinic Gino told me to show up the next day at the boxing gym at Harrison Park and said he would work with me," Scott remembered. "Gino mentored me on all aspects of refereeing and eventually allowed me to work the preliminary rounds of the Chicago Gloves tournament my first year."

Scott spent most weekends honing his skills on the local amateur circuit, and eventually refereed the championship bouts at the Golden Gloves tournament.

Illinois boxing commissioner Frank Glienna approached Scott a few years later at an amateur show about joining the paid ranks. He was impressed with Scott's fluid movement in the ring and ability to control the match.

Scott's coming out party was at a pro show in Kewanee, Illinois, on June 7, 1997. The card was in a small town hall and the crowd was there to see local heavyweight prospect Troy "The Country Boy" Weida. Scott had gone there to act as a judge, but the boxing commissioner tapped him to referee one of the preliminary bouts on the card.

"It was a packed house," he recollected, "and I remember feeling a little nervous when I climbed through the ropes. But my fight went off without a problem, and when it was over I changed clothes and came back to judge the main event!"

It wasn't long before Scott was refereeing main events. When 1992 U.S. Olympian Montell Griffin returned to Chicago after losing his WBC light heavyweight title to Roy Jones Jr., Scott refereed his comeback fight. "I know a lot of the boxers that I am refereeing from the local amateur scene," Scott said. "But once we get in the ring, everybody is the same. I completely cut myself off from ever making friends with any of the fighters."

In 2001, Gerald started working title fights, including O'Neil Bell's eleventh-round stoppage of Jose Luis Rivera for the North American Boxing Federation cruiserweight title. The fight was on a sweltering night in East St. Louis, Illinois, and the heat was almost as tough on the referee as it was on the fighters. "I must have lost five pounds that night in the ring," remembered Scott.

Scott literally almost lost his head the night he disqualified journeyman Arturo Velazquez in the first round for low blows and excessive holding in a bout against 1996 U.S. Olympic alternate Ramases Patterson. After repeated warnings Velazquez continued his illegal behavior, leaving Scott no alternative but to stop the fight. As the upset Velazquez left the ring he picked up a chair and hurled it over the ropes at Scott. It missed, and it was the last time Velazquez was seen in a Chicago area boxing ring.

When Scott refereed a 2001 preliminary bout at the rundown Fiesta Palace in Waukegan between Milwaukee club fighter Doug Brown and undefeated prospect Nick Cook, there were problems before the opening bell sounded. The ring announcer called the boxers to ring center and announced that it would be a four-round fight, whereupon Cook and his manager stormed out of the ring because they insisted that Cook had signed for a six-round fight. Scott stood waiting under the hot ring lights as Cook and his handler argued with the promoter and the crowd got increasingly restless. Eventually Cook was persuaded to return to the ring, and he made the issue of his contractual obligation moot by stopping Brown in the second round.

While there has not been any serious injury to a fighter in any contest arbitrated by Scott, Chicago boxer Francisco "Paco" Rodriguez, whom Scott refereed in the amateurs and several times as a pro, died tragically following his twelve-round bout with Tom Kennedy for the United States Boxing Association title in Philadelphia on November 20, 2009, at the Blue Horizon.

Rodriguez was a former national Golden Gloves champion and a rising professional prospect. Scott refereed seven of Rodriguez's professional bouts, including the Illinois state title match, which he won by knockout victory. "Francisco was a tough fighter and a humble young man," Scott recalled. "I first met him in the amateurs when I refereed several of his bouts. He was always very respectful, 'Yes sir, Mr. Scott,' 'Hello, Mr. Scott.' I attended his funeral and saw a photo of myself holding Francisco's hand up high after a victory. It really touched me and stayed with me for a long time."

Before each fight he works, "I say a prayer that I do a fair job for all concerned and especially that no one gets seriously hurt," Scott said. "Lord knows, if anything ever happened to a boxer when I was the referee it would bother me forever. Sometimes it is a referee's job to protect a fighter from himself. Some fighters will go on until they can't go no more. There's no quit in a lot of these warriors. As a referee sometimes we need to stop a bout regardless if the boxer still wants to continue, and we can't be concerned if there is a complaint that a bout has been stopped too soon."

Boxers of all sorts and skill levels form a professional boxing card, and Scott eagerly accepts all assignments the commission sends his way. On June 12, 2003, he officiated a bout involving Frankie "The Surgeon" Randall, the first boxer to defeat the legendary Julio Cesar Chavez. Randall, whose own skills were fading fast by then, pulled out a split-decision in a six rounder with little-known Patrick Thorns.

While he has never met anyone he hasn't liked in boxing, Scott is always careful to keep it strictly on a professional basis with the fighters inside and outside the ring. "As a referee, I always make sure that I don't get to be close friends with any of the boxers," he stated.

Sometimes it's hard, as in the case of Art Binkowski, the heavyweight who represented Canada in the 2000 Olympics and then turned professional (and later portrayed 1930s boxer John "Corn" Griffin in the movie *Cinderella Man*, starring Russell Crowe as heavyweight champion James J. Braddock). "Every time I saw Art at the fights in Chicago, he always went out of his way to say hello," recalled Scott, "and he always told me that I was a great referee. How do you not like a guy like that? But it's important to keep it professional at all times. A referee can have no favorites inside the ring."

Chicago has had numerous major fight cards in recent years, and Scott has worked many of the title contests. He has refereed bouts aired live on HBO, Showtime, and ESPN2, featuring talented boxers like Tomasz Adamek, Julio Cesar Chavez Jr., and Cory Spinks. "I don't pay attention to the television cameras," he said. "All I see are the two guys in the ring during the round and the three judges that I collect the scorecards from between rounds. However, I do tape all the televised telecasts I referee and view them several times to critique myself and pick up anything I could do to improve as a referee."

Beer-drinking, chain-smoking welterweight brawler Ricardo Mayorga defeated Michele Piccirillo in a pay-per-view event promoted by Don King in Chicago on August 13, 2005. Scott was the referee. Mayorga's reputation as an undisciplined loose cannon preceded him, but Scott had no problems with the free-swinging slugger from Nicaragua. "It was a good fight," he remembered. "Mayorga listened to my instructions without incident. In the fourth round I needed to bring both boxers to the ring center and warn them for hitting each other behind the head and to keep it clean, but that was it."

After being awarded the decision, Mayorga even sought out Scott, hugged him, and told him that he was a good referee.

Scott has worked several title fights promoted by Don King, and they have seen one another at boxing conventions. "We don't rub shoulders," said Scott. "As a referee, my job is to stay neutral. I don't mingle with promoters or boxers. Other than saying, 'It was a good bout,' to the fighters, I don't talk to them unless I have to."

On March 28, 2008, Scott was assigned to work the first boxing card aired live on the Internet by King on his own Web-TV station, www .donkingtv.com. The IBF light middleweight world title contest in St. Louis pitted champion and local hero Cory Spinks against crafty veteran Verno Phillips. Spinks lost his belt to Phillips on a split-decision.

Three years later, while attending the annual IBF convention in Las Vegas, Scott visited the Gold and Silver Pawn Shop, familiar to viewers of the top-rated History Channel show *Pawn Stars*. Cory Spinks's IBF championship belt was on display—possibly the very one that had been on the line in his fight against Phillips. Scott was jolted and saddened to see such a prized memento for sale in a pawnshop.

"I hope he got a lot of money for it," he said.

29

Steve Smoger

On the eve of his refereeing debut in Australia in November 2011, Steve Smoger bodysurfed under a blue sky in the Indian Ocean off the coast of Perth. Sirens had sounded when a great white shark was spotted in the area the day before, but Smoger, who grew up within blocks of the Atlantic Ocean in Atlantic City, wasn't fazed. Australia was the only continent outside Antarctica where he hadn't yet refereed a boxing match, and no mere shark was going to deprive him of the long-awaited opportunity of officiating or bodysurfing.

His long, successful boxing journey started on the couch in the Smoger house when Steve was just a kid. "My dad had always been a knowledgeable boxing fan," he said. "I remember watching the *Gillette Cavalcade of Sports* with him on Friday nights. Watching Archie Moore vs. Yvon Durelle in 1958 turned me on to boxing. It proved what my dad used to say about the sport: 'Boxers are the true athletes.' It's one-on-one, where the will and skill of one man must prevail over the other. There's no timeouts, and for three minutes it's just you and the other guy."

After a few amateur bouts, Smoger attended Penn State University and boxed in the intramural program. He continued to train while attending law school at the National Law Center (a division of The George Washington University in Washington, D.C.). When Smoger relocated back to New

Jersey he met Pat Duffy, who ran the legendary amateur ring program on the East Coast and was manager of the 1968 U.S. boxing team at the Olympic Games in Mexico City. Duffy was the one who had handed George Foreman the small American flag he famously waved to the crowd after becoming the Olympic heavyweight gold medalist.

When Smoger expressed interest in becoming an amateur boxing official, Duffy invited him to help with his next card, on the condition that Smoger be willing to learn "from the ground up" everything there was to know about running an amateur boxing show. Smoger eagerly agreed and reported for duty promptly at 5 p.m. at the next Atlantic City show as instructed.

"I remember walking into the Union Hall decked out in the all-white apparel required for officials of amateur boxing, and there was no ring set up," Smoger recalled. "Then Duffy handed me a broom and said, 'Start sweeping!' Nobody can say I didn't start from the ground up as an official!"

Smoger started as a timekeeper for the bouts, and gradually moved up to become an amateur judge and referee. Duffy sent him to Philadelphia to work with the Cappuccino brothers, Frank and Vic, both world-class professional referees. Smoger also trained with Zach Clayton, the legendary referee who was third man in the ring for the historic Muhammad Ali vs. George Foreman "Rumble in the Jungle" heavyweight title fight in Zaire. "Zach taught me a how to be smooth in the ring," he said. "He taught me some rhythm and how to move around."

By 1978, Smoger was employed as an assistant prosecutor in Atlantic City and was spending his free time in the ring at the Police Athletic League (PAL) Center working sparring matches for the pros who trained there. One day the gym's phone rang, and when nobody else picked it up Smoger did. The caller was then–New Jersey boxing commissioner Jersey Joe Walcott, the former world heavyweight champion, who was looking for someone to work as an inspector for several upcoming pro cards. "The following week I was assigned to a pro show at Resorts International, and it went from there," said Smoger.

A big boom in pro boxing was underway in Atlantic City, and as he worked as an inspector for the commission for the next few years, Smoger made sure Walcott and the other commissioners knew about his interest in donning the coveted bow tie. Finally Jersey Joe himself presented Smoger with his referee's license and he made his pro debut on a card at the Tropicana on September 23, 1982.

Exactly thirty years earlier, Walcott had lost his heavyweight title to Rocky Marciano by knockout in thirteen rounds. "I had mentioned to Jersey Joe that I had listened to that fight sitting on my dad's lap, and how upset I was when he was knocked out because we lived in New Jersey, too, and that I started crying and wailing," recalled Smoger. "Joe smiled and said that he'd had almost the exact same reaction."

As his career in the pro ring took off, so did Smoger's legal career. He became the first full-time prosecutor in Atlantic City, and in 1991 he was appointed to the Municipal Court bench.

In that era more than 150 pro cards were held in Atlantic City in the course of a single year. Smoger refereed at least two casino shows a week, handling bouts involving such contenders and future champions as Carl "The Truth" Williams, Virgil Hill, Micky Ward, and Lennox Lewis.

What Smoger refers to as his "coming-out party" occurred on April 23, 1988, in Pas-de-Calais, France, when Simon Brown battled Tyrone Trice for the vacant International Boxing Federation welterweight title. "It was a scheduled fifteen-round fight, and Trice was knocked down hard in the ninth and barely beat the count," recalled Smoger. "I let him continue and Trice came back and fought his heart out for five more rounds before I stopped the bout in the fourteenth round to spare him further punishment. Trice's fighting spirit was a sight to behold. Later that fight was voted the IBF's 'Fight of the Year.'"

Televised back in the United States by CBS, the first Brown vs. Trice fight gave American fans their first glimpse of Smoger, and they liked what they saw. With that fight his reputation as a fan's referee who "lets them fight" was launched.

Letting fighters fight is what a referee is supposed to do, Smoger said. "The less I interfere in a fight, the better chance it will be a more exciting fight for the viewers," he said. "People don't pay big dollars for ringside seats to watch the referee constantly break the fighters. I try to let the fight take its natural progression. If the rules are broken, or if a fighter is hurt, or if the boxers must be separated, I'll step in. But my philosophy is that the less I interfere, the better the fight will be."

A highlight of Smoger's career came in 1991, after he refereed a World Boxing Organization lightweight title fight in Johannesburg, South Africa, between local idol Dingaan Thobela, the champion, and Puerto Rico's tough Antonio Rivera. "Rivera caught Thobela with a hard punch early in the fight and really hurt him," Smoger recalled. "Then the pro-Thobela crowd that filled the stadium started singing a patriotic African song, and the effect was electric. Suddenly Thobela came back to life, and he went on to post a unanimous decision victory."

The day after fight, Smoger was invited to a luncheon for boxing officials. Seated at the head table was Nelson Mandela, who had been freed the previous year after twenty-seven years as a political prisoner in South Africa for his stand against apartheid. He was then and still remains one of the world's most revered figures. "I walked over and two bodyguards jumped up and put their hands near their guns," remembered Smoger. "'It's okay,' Mandela told them, 'he is the referee of the boxing match last night.' We spoke for several minutes, and Mr. Mandela said, 'You did a fine job in the fight, young man.' I told him that coming from a former boxer, which Mr. Mandela was, that was a real compliment."

Back in Atlantic City, Smoger told the mayor about meeting Mandela. "He was so impressed that he asked me to talk about the experience before the Chamber of Commerce," he said. "When he introduced me to the crowd of four hundred local movers and shakers, the mayor shook my hand and proclaimed how proud he was to 'shake the hand that had shaken Nelson Mandela's hand!' That's an example of the cultural side of the boxing industry that few people realize we see as international officials."

Smoger met the King of Thailand when he worked two fights in Bangkok featuring Khaosai Galaxy. Khaosai and his brother, Khaokor, were the only twin brothers to become world boxing champions. It was in the late 1980s, and Smoger was fascinated by the adulation heaped on the fighting brothers. "Khaosai had a special pre-fight routine that was described in rapturous detail by a battery of reporters who followed his every move," remembered Smoger. "A private cook prepared his meals, and there was a very intense pre-fight prayer ceremony, as if Galaxy was being anointed to single-handedly defend the country from disaster."

Some things that happen during a fight aren't covered by the rulebook, as Smoger found out when he refereed the World Boxing Association light heavyweight title fight between champion Virgil Hill and Adolpho Washington on February 20, 1993. "In round ten or eleven, Washington sustained a severe cut over his right eye," recalled Smoger "Between rounds the doctor came in to look at it. The fight was being televised, and the cameraman was in the corner. I told him to get the camera out of there because he was impeding the doctor, and as the guy spun the camera around it caught Washington and inflicted a cut over his left eye! Virgil was ahead on points, and was awarded a Technical Decision victory. It was one strange situation."

Refereeing can be hazardous to one's health, as Smoger has learned the hard way several times. During the Carl "The Truth" Williams vs. Tim Witherspoon fight in Atlantic City in 1991, Williams threw a punch that caught Smoger in the back of his head. "I saw stars! But I moved a bit away from the boxers and circled to clear my head and continued to monitor the action."

In 1999, Smoger was seated ringside acting as knockdown timekeeper for the Hasim Rahman vs. Oleg Maskaev I fight in Atlantic City. In the eighth round, Rahman was punched out of the ring and landed on the table near Steve. He was counted out. A spectator seated in the balcony expressed his disappointment with the result by picking up his chair and heaving it toward the ring. The chair hit Smoger in the head.

"I thought that the ceiling caved in," he remembered. "I didn't know what hit me. The ringside physician told me later that if the impact of the chair had hit me more directly that I could have been killed. As it was, my jaw was shut for almost a week from the blow. I had to suck chicken noodle soup from a straw. Years later they found the guy who tossed the chair, but I didn't press charges."

The first major sporting event in New York City after the terrorist attacks on the World Trade Center on September 11, 2001, was Bernard Hopkins's middleweight title unification match against Felix "Tito" Trinidad at

Madison Square Garden on September 29. The bout had been scheduled for September 15, but was postponed after the tragedy that killed nearly three thousand people.

Smoger was the referee, and later recalled the emotional atmosphere in a December 25, 2011, interview with Michael Schmidt of www.boxing.com, titled "Steve Smoger: Master of an Art Form": "They had a substantial number of firefighters in a special section that promoter Don King had set up," said Smoger, "he had donated a large amount of money towards fire equipment for Engine #10, across the street from the South Tower. And then Jimmy Lennon got the ten-count voiced in for as I remember it emotionally set out for 'the victims, the heroes and the Nation.' The place was in tears."

As for the fight, Steve stated that when Trinidad hit Hopkins on the jaw with a solid shot in the sixth or seventh round, "Bernard shrugged and fired back. The look on Tito's face said, *Oh, shit! It is going to be a long night!* It was a dominant performance for Hopkins, but Tito's fighting heart kept him in the fight until his corner threw in the towel in the twelfth and final round."

Two weeks later, Smoger was in Copenhagen, Denmark, to referee Mike Tyson's bout against Danish hero "Super" Brian Nielsen. A win for Tyson would secure a mega-fight against universally recognized heavyweight champion Lennox Lewis.

"In Tyson's previous fight he knocked out Lou Savarese in Scotland, and gave the referee, my friend John Coyle, all kinds of problems," recalled Smoger. "Tyson actually hit Coyle and knocked him down as Coyle was trying to pull him off Savarese. I wanted to make sure that this wouldn't happen to me, so I asked Tyson's manager, Shelly Finkel, if I could have a few words with Tyson man-to-man before the fight.

"I began by saying that I had always been a big fan of his and that I thought the job he had done to bring energy and fans back to boxing was a huge plus for the sport," said Smoger of the pre-fight meeting in Tyson's dressing room. "I reminded Mike that if he won the fight he would face Lennox Lewis in one of history's most anticipated heavyweight title fights. I told him that I respected him and expected in return his respect in the ring, and pointed out that forty thousand fans had paid to see a clean fight. With each comment, Tyson nodded in agreement, and at the end of what was the most intense pre-fight instructional I ever had, he looked directly at me and said, 'Steve, I understand, and you will have no problems with me tonight.'"

Which is how it worked out, although at the close of the sixth round Tyson cocked his hand to throw a punch just as the bell rang. "We made eye contact at that very moment," remembered Smoger, "and to his credit, Tyson didn't throw the punch. After the seventh round Nielsen complained of double vision. When I held up two fingers and he said he saw four, I stopped the fight."

Enforcing the rules is a referee's job, but Smoger allows some leeway for the sake of a good, entertaining bout. He cites Vinny Pazienza and Emanuel "The Drunken Master" Augustus as examples of fighters whose unique personas and styles warranted extra latitude. "Augustus would do what he called the 'String-Puppet Dance' during his bouts, and he sometimes punched with both hands simultaneously," Smoger recalled with a laugh. "I remember seeing a bout in which Augustus was penalized a point for spinning out of a clinch, even though it was not against the rules. He just liked to showboat. I would never go out of my way to hamper boxers who like to show off a bit, as long as their antics don't violate any rules. In 2001, I refereed Augustus's ten-round war with Micky Ward in New Hampshire. I stayed out of their way, and later *The Ring* magazine voted it Fight of the Year."

In 2007, Smoger refereed another Fight of the Year. This one was a World Boxing Council middleweight title eliminator between Kelly Pavlik and Edison Miranda in Memphis, Tennessee. "What tough guys they were," he said. "In round four, Miranda hit Pavlik on the button with two solid right hands, and when Pavlik didn't even flinch I thought to myself, *How can he take those kinds of punches without being affected?* Two rounds later, Pavlik dropped Miranda, and he finished him off in the seventh round."

Two months after that fight, Smoger attended a medical seminar conducted by Dr. Anthony Alessi, one of the most highly respected neurologists in the fight game. "Dr. Alessi explained how a hard punch that lands behind the ear or in the temple area can have an immediate but not long-lasting adverse effect on a boxer's equilibrium," said Smoger. "He discussed the punch taken by Zab Judah in his bout with Kostya Tszyu that sent Judah staggering awkwardly around the ring. When Dr. Alessi said that there may be an immediate effect from this type of punch but the recovery from it is usually very quick, that stuck with me.

"Two months later I refereed another Kelly Pavlik fight, this one against Jermaine Taylor for the WBC middleweight title. In round two, Taylor knocked down Pavlik with a hard left hand behind the ear, and Kelly looked to be in serious trouble. But my mind went back to the Miranda fight and I thought to myself that he might weather the storm. I never even considered stopping it. Pavlik got up at the count of eight on wobbly legs, and sure enough, he not only survived but came back to knock out Taylor in the seventh round.

"If I hadn't had the benefit of that recent medical seminar and what I already knew about Pavlik's strong recuperative powers," continued Smoger, "I might very well have stopped the fight in the second round. Letting it continue was the right call for the fight and for boxing.

"Fighters know that I have a strong respect for them, and they accord me the same respect," said Smoger. "The result of this is fewer interruptions in the fights I referee. For example, I did the Pawel Wolak vs. Delvin Rodriguez fight in New York on July 15, 2011, and I think I broke them up just once during the whole ten rounds. The fight was televised live on ESPN2, and the viewing audience saw a war, a candidate for Fight of the Year!"

Wolak vs. Rodriguez was later named the 2011 Boxing Writers Association of America Fight of the Year. It was the third time that Smoger had refereed a BWAA Fight of the Year, and he remains the only referee to hold that distinction.

30

Richard Steele

A man of honor and character, Richard Steele feels he owes a great deal to the sport of boxing. "It made me the man I am today," he stated. Boxing fans remember Richard Steele for his thirty-four years as a referee, most of them in Nevada, and the mega-fights that he worked. It is impossible to think of big-time boxing in Las Vegas in the '80s, '90s, and early 2000s—a Mike Tyson, Marvin Hagler, Sugar Ray Leonard, Larry Holmes, or Roberto Duran fight—without thinking of Steele.

But he is much more than a noted referee. "I have four kids, all four graduated from college, I have been married to my wife, Gladys, for over thirty years," said the Marine Corps veteran and family man, who has dedicated his life to helping youth in the Las Vegas area better themselves through boxing. "Life is wonderful."

Over the years, Steele has worn many hats in the sport—amateur and professional boxer, fight judge, referee, coach, manager, promoter, and, today, he runs the Richard Steele Health and Wellness Center in North Las Vegas. The gym targets at risk and underprivileged youth in the greater Las Vegas area.

On active duty from 1961 to 1966, Steele was a member of the Marine Corps boxing team from 1962 to 1965. One of his teammates was future

185

heavyweight Hall of Famer Ken Norton. Steele went on to a professional career as a light heavyweight, from 1966 to 1970, retiring with a record of 12-4, with ten knockouts. He fought mainly at the Olympic Auditorium, the famed boxing arena in his hometown of Los Angeles.

With his military and boxing careers in his background, it was not long before Steele moved to the next phase of his life, and was refereeing and judging boxing in California. Much as boxers from around the country would gravitate to Las Vegas to hone their craft, Steele eventually moved to that city to be able to work the big fights, he said. While in Vegas, he worked in gaming for over ten years, as a slot supervisor and a pit boss for casinos. Prior to that, he worked for the Gaming Control Board.

In his thirty-four years as a referee, Steele worked many of the most memorable fights of several eras, epic boxing matches like Aaron Pryor vs. Alexis Arguello II, Marvin Hagler vs. Thomas Hearns, Julio Cesar Chavez vs. Meldrick Taylor, Sugar Ray Leonard vs. Marvin Hagler, Sugar Ray Leonard vs. Thomas Hearns II, Larry Holmes vs. Leon Spinks, Mike Tyson vs. Donovan "Razor" Ruddock I, Ray Mancini vs. Bobby Chacon, Sugar Ray Leonard vs. Roberto Duran III, Iran Barkley vs. Thomas Hearns I, Oscar De La Hoya vs. Julio Cesar Chavez II, Floyd Mayweather Jr. vs. Zab Judah, Roy Jones Jr. vs. James Toney, Floyd Mayweather Jr. vs. Diego Corrales, Frankie Randall vs. Julio Cesar Chavez I, Steve Cruz vs. Barry McGuigan, Mike McCallum vs. Donald Curry, Hector Camacho vs. Rafael "Bazooka" Limon, Bobby Chacon vs. Cornelius Boza-Edwards II, and Paulie Ayala vs. Johnny Tapia II.

Steele also was the third man in the ring for fights involving Lupe Pintor, Carlos Zarate, Wilfred Benitez, Juan Manuel Marquez, Marco Antonio Barrera, Felix Trinidad, Azumah Nelson, Terry Norris, Nigel Benn, Riddick Bowe, Evander Holyfield, Michael Carbajal, Lennox Lewis, Ricardo Lopez, and Kostya Tszyu.

In 1999, Steele went to Quezon City, outside Manila, in the Philippines to referee the first title defense of a then little-known 112-pound World Boxing Council flyweight champion Manny Pacquiao. Pacquiao won by fourth-round technical knockout over his obscure Mexican challenger, Gabriel Mira, and would go on to become one of boxing's greatest superstars.

Although he achieved fame for his role as the third man in the ring in many of boxing's most memorable contests, Steele was also a very accomplished judge. The most high-profile contest he judged was the October 2, 1980, contest at Caesars Palace between Larry Holmes and "The Greatest" Muhammad Ali, who was fighting in a comeback and trying to win the heavyweight title from his former sparring partner. Holmes reluctantly gave Ali a battering for ten rounds before Ali's corner stopped the fight.

Steele also judged bouts featuring top notch boxers Jung-Koo Chang, Azumah Nelson, Bobby Chacon, Carlos Palomino, Alberto Davila, Danny Lopez, and Ruben Olivares.

The last title fight that Steele worked was on August 12, 2006. David Diaz won the interim WBC lightweight title against Jose Armando Santa Cruz by a come-from-behind-knockout in the tenth round. His last major fight was the April 8, 2006, IBF welterweight title fight between Floyd Mayweather Jr. and Zab Judah. Mayweather won a twelve-round decision. Steele knew that after working the fight that it was time to leave.

"I decided I wanted to leave on top," said Steele. "Mayweather vs. Judah was a big fight, and there was no controversy to the ending or outcome. That's about as good as it gets, so I decided to retire."

One of the most regrettable things people can't seem to forget about Steele's refereeing career is the March 17, 1990, fight he refereed between Julio Cesar Chavez and Meldrick Taylor. As the August 2, 2010, article on Steele in *Sports Illustrated* by Julia Morrill stated, "His thirty-four year career is defined by a two second call." The fight between the two greats was a classic. Julio Cesar Chavez was one of the greatest fighters ever to come from boxing-rich Mexico. He was 68-0, held the WBC light welterweight title, and had also won titles at junior lightweight and lightweight. Taylor was 24-0-1 and held the IBF 140 pound title. He had won the gold medal in the featherweight division for the United States in the 1984 Los Angeles Olympics at seventeen years of age. The two were among boxing's top pound-for-pound fighters. Taylor could hit, but he was considered the speedy boxer. Chavez had excellent skills and could box but was considered the aggressive slugger.

Chavez was behind on the scores after eleven rounds. The cards read 107–102, 108–101, Taylor, and 105–104, Chavez. Taylor was landing far more punches, but Chavez's harder shots were causing more damage. With under a minute left in the fight, Chavez staggered Taylor badly, following it up with a series of damaging blows, and flooring him with a right. Taylor got up, but failed to respond when Steele asked him if he was okay. Steele stopped the fight with two seconds left to go. A chorus of boos erupted. Steele was criticized by some and lauded by others. Taylor was hospitalized after the fight—he had sustained a facial fracture, was urinating blood, and had lost more than two pints of blood.

Taylor went on to win other titles, but was never the same fighter after the loss. He continued to fight for small purses until 2002, when he retired, broke and in legal trouble. In 2003 Taylor was featured in an episode of HBO's stunning *Legendary Nights*, "The Tale of Chavez vs. Taylor." The episode showed a horrifically brain damaged thirty-six-year-old Taylor, speaking in an unintelligible whisper, requiring subtitles to understand his speech. Steele remembers receiving letters, people calling his house, and getting threats after the fight. But he has always insisted that he made the right decision, and would do the same today.

"I asked him if he was okay. He couldn't speak to me. Once a fighter is battered into that condition, where he couldn't speak, the fight is over, no matter what time it is," related Steele. "The time makes no difference. He [Meldrick Taylor] was a great fighter, and he was winning. But Chavez was doing more damage. Taylor was landing those pitty-pat punches. At the end of the fight, Taylor was a beaten, battered fighter. It is a shame a guy takes that much punishment."

For years after, there would be fans that would boo him every time he was announced as the third man in the ring. "It was difficult," Steele admits. "But you learn in life, and things make you tougher. I have learned in life that in tougher incidents, you have to stand in your beliefs. That has helped make me the person I am today. It was tough. But I know I did the right thing.

"The guy can't even speak today, you cannot understand him," said Steele, reflecting on Taylor's episode of *Legendary Nights*. "He was in the hospital for a week. The way he is now, I know I did the right thing. The thing about a lot of these corner people, they are just thinking about the win. They are not considering the fighters, their long-term health. They are not looking at life after boxing, or if [a fighter] will be able to enjoy a life after boxing."

Steele should not be remembered for two seconds of a boxing career. If there is an official synonymous with boxing greatness, it is Richard Steele. The Nevada commission put great faith in him, and he was given a substantial percentage of their biggest fights. Steele refereed *The Ring* magazine's 1983 Fight of the Year, Bobby Chacon vs. Cornelius Boza Edwards II; the 1985 Fight of the Year, Marvin Hagler vs. Thomas Hearns; the 1986 Fight of the Year, Steve Cruz vs. Barry McGuigan; the 1987 Fight of the Year, Sugar Ray Leonard vs. Marvin Hagler; and the 1990 Fight of the Year, Chavez vs. Taylor

Marvin Hagler's three-round shootout with Thomas Hearns—Hagler won by third round knockout—is listed as the number two fight of all time by *Men's Fitness* magazine, the number seven title fight of all time by *The Ring* magazine, the number seven fight of all time by *Time* magazine, and the number nine fight of all time by *Sports Illustrated*. Julio Cesar Chavez's twelfth round technical knockout over Meldrick Taylor is listed as the number six fight of all time by *Men's Fitness*, the number nine fight by *Time*, the thirteenth greatest fight of all time by *The Ring*. It was also *The Ring*'s Fight of the Decade at the end of the 1990s.

Five other fights refereed by Steele appear on *The Ring*'s list of the top one hundred title fights of all time—Chacon-Boza vs. Edwards II (#22), Iran Barkley's knockout of Thomas Hearns (#53), unheralded Steve Cruz's decision win over potential Irish superstar Barry McGuigan (#82), Frankie Randall's stunning twelve round upset decision win over 89-0-1 Julio Cesar Chavez in January 1994 (#85), and Leonard vs. Hagler (#88).

In 2003, the award-winning HBO documentary series *Legendary Nights* featured twelve episodes, each of which highlighted the most significant boxing rivalries that had been televised either on HBO or HBO pay-per-view. Steele had refereed four of those rivalries: Leonard vs. Hagler, Hagler vs. Hearns, Chavez vs. Taylor, and Aaron Pryor vs. Alexis Arguello. Steele has had quite a career, and now he sees his role as giving something back through work at his gym. "Boxing has been good to me. I went to school, but I dropped out [of high school]. Because of boxing, I graduated from high school and junior college," reflected Steele. "Boxing is a way to prepare one's self for the world. We have about two hundred and fifty kids in the gym. We have tutors come over from UNLV [the University of Nevada at Las Vegas] to teach the kids. We have police come here, and give classes two times a week on bullying and gangs. If this can be a way to prevent kids from using alcohol, drugs, and tobacco, then it is a good thing. Today, we not only have boxing, but we also have MMA, because the young kids like that."

He talked about his work at the gym with kids in the north Las Vegas area in a November 22, 2000, article by Todd Dewey in the *Las Vegas Review Journal*, "Boxing is the carrot that brings them in, but once I get them here, it's my duty as a Christian to try to help them, not only in boxing, but in everyday life." Steele also occasionally promotes MMA. "I did promote boxing for a while," he said. "But that is too tough these days, with most of the fighters tied up in long-term contracts with promoters." Steele's wife, Gladys, has also managed boxers over the years.

"I am proud that my wife has managed three fighters who ended up fighting for the world title. She managed Michael Grant at the start of his career," said Steele of the heavyweight giant and former football and basketball standout whose title challenge dreams were shattered in a second-round knockout loss to Lennox Lewis in 2000, going down four times in that bout. "She also managed David Sample and Ross Thompson. I fought with Ross's dad in the Marines."

Richard Steele may be retired from refereeing, but he is still in the gym, still coaching. "I am still a fan. I still follow the fights. We often have parties at the gym for the kids, so they can see the big boxing matches."

Richard Steele has had his ups and downs, but the Marine veteran has been made tougher by life's lessons. "Boxing has been so good to me. If I can pass that along, and teach these kids to take care of themselves, to stay away from gangs, from harm, to get a good education, then I have done my job."

31

Mickey Vann

Recognized as one of the game's premier referees, Mickey Vann is always strictly business when he's between the ropes. But it's a different story when he's not. The gregarious Englishman makes it a point to have fun and enjoy himself to the utmost, which was certainly the case when Vann was on an airplane headed for a refereeing assignment in Italy in 1996.

During the flight, he struck up a conversation with a gorgeous young woman from Japan who was escorting a group of Japanese tourists around Europe.

As he wrote in his autobiography, *Give Me a Ring*, Vann eventually made a pass. "What a pity I'm not staying over in Rome," he said. "I think if I were, we would sleep together."

When the woman smiled, instead of shrieking and looking for a parachute, Vann pressed on. "Do you know what the Mile High Club is?" he inquired. She did, and by the time the plane landed they were both members.

"As I changed planes in Rome," he continued, "I bumped into her party again. All the Japanese guys were pointing at me and laughing. So much for the discretion of Oriental women!"

That kind of boldness has made Vann one of England's most accomplished referees. A veteran of thirty-plus years in boxing, he has refereed bouts featuring British greats Ricky Hatton, "Prince" Naseem Hamed, and Joe Calzaghe, along with world title fights in several countries abroad. His career reached its zenith when he arbitrated the historic bout between Lennox Lewis and Frank Bruno in Cardiff, Wales, on October 1, 1993. Dubbed "The Battle of Britain," it was the first time two Englishmen battled each other for the world heavyweight title. More than ninety million people viewed the bout worldwide.

The spotlight has been Vann's home from an early age. Born Michael Van Norman in south London in 1943, Mickey grew up as part of his father's circus show, appearing as "The Giraffe-Necked Woman" or a stooge for the clowns; he even did a short stint on the trapeze. His father went by the stage name of Hal Denver, and Mickey idolized him. Denver was best known for his knife-throwing act and once hurled a blade at Gwen Major, mother of British prime minister John Major. Denver performed his act in the United States and even appeared on the *Ed Sullivan Show* with Elvis Presley, with whom he formed a strong friendship.

Vann's grandfather, Tom Norman, actually started the family in show business. He traveled throughout England exhibiting human oddities, the most noteworthy being a deformed man named Joseph Merrick, better known to the world as the "Elephant Man."

Vann's parents split up early in his life, and as a result his youth was divided between traveling with his father's circus and bouncing around various foster homes whenever his dad choose to leave him behind. "I received no formal education from ages seven to thirteen," he remembered. "My education consisted of my mum making me read and write three times a week for an hour." But he got quite an education in life. By the time he was thirteen, Vann was one of England's best ballroom dancers and showed talent at gymnastics and soccer. While traveling around with the circus he also developed an abiding interest in boxing, disappointing his father who had hoped Mickey would become a knife-thrower, too.

After an argument with his father, Vann went out on his own for good at fourteen. He initially slept on park benches and survived by doing odd jobs in Leeds. He also pursued his interest in boxing, competing in sixty-six amateur contests as a member of the Market and District Boy's Club.

While still a teenager, Vann married and became a father. Needing to supplement his income from a nightshift job in a factory, he decided to turn pro. He beat Ronnie McCulloch by decision in his first paid fight in 1969, and in the next year defeated British title contenders Bernie Nichols and Mickey Lynch. He was a decent boxer but often resorted to pure slugging with his opponents. "I'd decide to get into a tear-up, and before I knew it I'd be sitting on my backside," he told the *Yorkshire Evening Post* in a December 18, 2008, article "Mickey Vann: Everyday Has Been Like Christmas for Me." Another problem was that he didn't train properly and often took fights on short notice, and so ended up losing more than he won in his career.

At age twenty-nine, Vann realized he wasn't headed anywhere as a boxer and retired from the ring. But he soon missed the sport and decided to make a return to the ring in a less painful capacity. He contacted his former manager, Tommy Miller, for assistance in getting started as a trainer. Given his lack of success as a fighter, Miller doubted that Vann would make a good instructor of the sweet science and suggested that he consider becoming a referee instead.

In Great Britain, boxing is governed by the British Boxing Board of Control (BBBC), an authority that demands much of its licensed apprentice referees. Vann started out by memorizing the rule book and then spent eighteen months traveling at his own expense to pro shows, judging the fights and observing the referees in action. His first assignment as third man in the ring was to work a few preliminary bouts under the direction of Wally Thom, an experienced and highly respected arbiter who'd earned the exalted status of Star Grade Referee.

His very first outing was far from stellar. The custom then in all British fights was for the referee to act as sole judge and proclaim the winner of a fight. Since Vann was just an apprentice, the actual decisions would be made by Thom at ringside and transmitted to Vann.

The fight went the distance, and at its conclusion Vann motioned for both boxers to come to the center of the ring for the decision. Then he raised the hand of the wrong boxer. The crowd started to boo, and the real winner was hastily anointed. Vann was humiliated and thought his career as a referee was over after just one fight. But it wasn't, and in Vann's next outing he got a little help from veteran referee Wally Thom.

"I don't know if he felt responsible for the previous fiasco, but [Thom] was terrific," Vann later wrote in his autobiography. "He always used to have a little nip to steady his nerves before he got into the ring, and he decided that is what I needed. So he took me to the bar, where I had three or four, and I sailed through the fight, even managing to lift the correct arm this time."

He kept on lifting the correct arms after that, and Vann's new career took off. He became one of only three licensed referees in his area and received assignments to work on a regular basis.

Within a few years Vann advanced to an A-grade status official, which would allow him to referee any contest below a British Championship bout. Eight years after his embarrassing debut, Vann achieved the status of Star-Grade referee. The downside was that because all the travel involved, his marriage disintegrated. So he threw himself into his work even harder, always willing to take a last-minute call to a far off destination.

Some of the world title assignments he took were to enjoyable venues in Argentina and Japan, but others landed Vann in some very risky outposts. One of them was Lusaka, Zambia, where Mickey went a few days before Christmas of 1990 to referee a fight for the WBC International light heavy-weight title involving Zambian national hero Lottie Mwale.

Lusaka was an overpopulated, filthy, crime-ridden city, and Vann needed security guards to escort him whenever he left his hotel. When he arrived at the arena, the first thing Vann noticed was that there was no padding beneath the apron of the ring, a dangerous situation for the fight-ers. Taking the matter into his own hands, he went into the arena's business office, tore up its carpeting, and used it to pad the apron just minutes before the TV cameras went on for the fight's live broadcast.

Vann views all his boxing travels and travails in a positive light (even when they don't involve unexpected convocations of the Mile High Club). "When you turn up at an airport and there's no one there to pick you up, and you don't have a clue where you're supposed to be going, it's an adven-ture," Vann said to the *Yorkshire Evening Post* on August 22, 2010.

Some adventures he could have done without, like the time he was physically attacked by the father of a fighter after Vann had stopped the son's
match to save him from further punishment. But overall, he said, "I have
loved every moment of it. Some are better than others, but I have enjoyed
it all."

When he was assigned as the third man in the ring for "The Battle of
Britain" between Lewis and Bruno, Vann couldn't have been more proud.
"You can't get any better than the heavyweight championship of the world,"
he said. "I think there was a television audience of ninety-one or ninety-two
million, and in the stadium they were singing 'Land of Hope and Glory,'
and fireworks went off around the stadium, and I was there in the middle
of the ring, with the rain coming down, ready to referee one of Britain's
most historic boxing matches."

Bruno was the aggressor early and rocked Lewis in the third round with
a right hand. After six rounds Bruno held a slight edge on the scorecards of
two of the judges. But the tide changed in the seventh when Lewis landed
a pulverizing left hook from which Bruno couldn't recover, and Vann
stopped the contest in the champion's favor.

A good knowledge of boxing and plain common sense are the main
tools a referee needs, he believes. Vann does not favor the rule that calls for
a referee to stop the fight if a fighter has been knocked down three times in
a single round. That should be a discretionary call for the referee to make,
he opines, using his common sense to appraise the situation. Mickey clas-
sified himself as an old-school referee in an April 14, 2008, interview with
the boxing website SecondsOut.com by Andre Wake titled "Giving Mickey
Vann a Ring." "I think the better referees are the ones that have been fighters," he said. "When you've fought yourself, you have a feeling for when a
fighter has had enough and when he wants to carry on. In championship
fights I like to give a fighter a chance without them getting hurt; if that
means they go on too long then so be it, it's a tough sport. I'd have died for
a chance to fight for a British title. I'd have gone down fighting, but it's different now, you don't get many like that."

Women's boxing gained a wider audience in the 1990s when Christy
Martin battled on pay-per-view as a prelude to a Mike Tyson heavyweight

title defense, and it seemed there was at least one female bout featured on every big card thereafter. Vann is not a supporter of female boxing, as he told SecondsOut.com. "There are so many things women can do in sport, they don't have to try and knock seven bells off each other," he said. "The problem is that women see men do sports and they think they should do it. There are many sports for them, but boxing isn't one of them. Boxing is a man's sport and some women think they are as good as men and they should do it. The only problem is that nobody wants to watch them. There's also a risk for the referee. What if you parted them and you touched one of their breasts? She could say, 'You assaulted me.' There was one fighter in America who fought when she was four months pregnant. It's wrong."

In 2008, Vann was forced into retirement in Britain by a Boxing Board of Control rule requiring all referees to turn in their licenses at the end of the year they turn sixty-five. "I don't agree with that," he said. "I think there should be a fitness test and if you are not good enough or you're not fit enough, then you should go."

Though Vann is still licensed by the Boxing Union of Ireland, enabling him to referee anywhere in the world except the Great Britain, he told SecondsOut.com that he misses working at home and "the calls from the Board asking, 'Mickey can you do this fight?' I'll miss getting ready for it and making sure I've got everything and the buzz leading up to the fight," he said. "And the people. I've met so many associates over the years, and I'll miss doing a job I know I'm good at [refereeing in Great Britain]." But he has the satisfaction of looking back on a great, acclaimed career.

"My dad would have been proud of me," continued Vann in the SecondsOut.com article. "He was my driving force. I've proved that if anybody wants something in life and they work hard enough, they can do it."

In 2010 *The Fighter*, a movie about the life of American welterweight contender Micky Ward, was nominated for the Best Picture Oscar. In the movie is a climactic scene from the bout between Ward and England's Shay Neary for the World Boxing Union title. The referee was an actor playing the role of Mickey Vann.

While still active as a referee in Ireland and occasionally abroad, Vann now spends the balance of his time as a conditioning coach for the Leeds

Rhinos Rugby League club. He also took Leeds City College to its first two national college finals, and has led other area rugby teams to titles.

Vann and his wife, Marie, whom he affectionately calls "his rock," also take foster children and juvenile delinquents into their home. He isn't working fifty weeks a year anymore, but life for Vann hasn't slowed down yet.

32

Tony Weeks

Al Munoz, the late, well-respected Arizona boxing official, once told Tony Weeks that "referees are not made, they are born." Perhaps that is the only way to explain the meteoric rise of Tony Weeks to the top of the boxing world. No other boxing referee has burst onto the world scene in quite the fashion that Weeks has.

Weeks has worked for the Federal Bureau of Prisons for more than twenty years. In 1993, he was the recreation supervisor at a federal correctional institution in Arizona. He arranged boxing matches for inmates, but one day no referee showed up. Weeks volunteered to act as the referee. Veteran Tucson trainer Beto Martinez, who was working with the prison boxers, observed Weeks in action and asked if he had done any refereeing before. Weeks had not. Martinez told Weeks he was a natural and could tell that he was talented, even though the bouts were only exhibitions.

Martinez told Arizona boxing commissioner John Montano about hiring Weeks to referee. "Martinez discovered me, and Montano gave me a shot," said Weeks, who became a licensed referee in 1994. "I had no amateur experience, no experience in boxing. I was in the right place at the right time."

The boxing bug caught Weeks in a major way. By 1996, Weeks had worked his first world title—a WBA title fight between Eloy Rojas and

Miguel Arrozal. In the next eighteen months, he would referee world title fights in Japan, South Korea, and Thailand.

Weeks requested a transfer to a federal prison closer to the Las Vegas area in 2000. He was sent to Victorville, California, where he still works, and is the recreation supervisor. "If you are going to pursue boxing, and that's what I did, Vegas is the place," related Weeks, who resides in Las Vegas.

Nevada is perhaps one of the hardest states for a person to become a professional boxing official in, due to the demand. But Weeks made the move a smooth one, transitioning quickly into major Las Vegas fights. But he recognizes that it may not be so easy for all officials.

"Start out slow, at the amateur level," Weeks recommends. "Go to a boxing gym, and ask the trainers if you can work sparring matches. Go up to them, and say, 'Do you mind if I work with the fighters?' Learn to stay in position. If you miss a call, you may be a step too late to stop the fight. You will grow, you will become more confident. You will get in bigger fights and be able to handle them."

"Anyone can be taught the rules and regulations. Not everyone can be taught the instincts to apply them," Weeks reflected. "That said, you must be mentally sharp. You must be able to function under extreme circumstances. You make split second decisions. You cannot be indecisive. You must be in good physical condition. There are two finely tuned athletes. You have to keep up with them." Weeks, a large, muscular man, is noted for having excellent footwork and positioning in the ring, and being able to move with the little men. "I still have a tape of that first fight I refereed," he said. "And I can still see 'me' in there. I have the same movement, I have learned, but I look the same."

Weeks has always been an athlete, with a background in football, track, and a variety of martial arts. "I am always working out, always hitting the gym," he said. "I do a lot of cardio for boxing, so I can keep up. I do light weights and high reps."

The move to Las Vegas reflected his devotion to boxing. He also learned Spanish. Many are surprised to hear Weeks, a non-Hispanic African American, speaking Spanish so well in the ring.

"I learned boxing Spanish at first. It was a tribute to Beto Martinez. Latinos started me in boxing. Then I started studying more, and learning more words. I have worked with a lot of Latin fighters. It has most definitely helped me. I have had an overwhelmingly positive response from the Latin community, as they see a non-Hispanic referee take the time to learn Spanish."

Weeks's dedication, athletic background, and experience in martial arts have also paid off in mixed martial arts (MMA). He is one of the most experienced MMA judges and has officiated in many major fights, such as Nick Diaz vs. B. J. Penn, Chuck Liddell vs. Wanderlei Silva, several Anderson Silva UFC title fights, and Shawn Sherk vs. Kenny Florian for the UFC lightweight title. He has traveled around the world to work UFC cards. "I think there is room for both sports. Boxing has been around for a long time," commented Weeks. "MMA is the fastest rising sport. It has a big fan base, but boxing will always be around."

Like any official, Weeks has had bumps in the road and learned from them. "My first really big fight was the night before the Felix 'Tito' Trinidad vs. Fernando Vargas fight," he said, referring to the classic pay-per-view battle on December 2, 2000. "The night before, I did Bernard Hopkins vs. Antwun Echols II. It was on HBO. That was a rough, tough, all-out street fight. In the midst of the fight, I kept thinking, *My career is over, I am done. Larry Merchant* [the HBO boxing announcer] *is probably having a field day.*"

The bout, a rematch of a tough Hopkins title defense, featured IBF middleweight champion Hopkins winning by a tenth round technical knockout over hard-hitting Echols. In the sixth round, Echols was deducted two points for body slamming Hopkins and dislocating his shoulder. In the seventh, Echols went down. In the eighth, Hopkins had a point taken off for hitting behind the head. "At the end of the fight, Marc Ratner [of the Nevada commission] pulled me aside, told me no interviews, and let me know it had been a tough fight," said Weeks. "Joe Cortez [the Hall of Fame veteran referee] told me that it was a rough bout, a hard fight for even the most experienced referees."

But it was not a career wrecker and Weeks kept rolling along, learning and getting better. Over the years, he has been entrusted to be the third man in such important matches as Manny Pacquiao vs. Juan Manuel Marquez III, Marcos Maidana vs. Erik Morales, Juan Manuel Lopez vs. Rafael Marquez, Bernard Hopkins vs. Roy Jones Jr. II, Floyd Mayweather Jr. vs. Juan Manuel Marquez, Wladimir Klitschko vs. Hasim Rahman, Manny Pacquiao vs. Oscar De La Hoya, Kelly Pavlik vs. Jermain Taylor II, Manny Pacquiao vs. Marco Antonio Barrera, Ronald "Winky" Wright vs. Shane Mosley, and Joel Casamayor vs. Diego Corrales. Weeks has also refereed bouts with boxers Brandon Rios, Jorge Arce, Roberto Guerrero, Ricky Hatton, Steve Cunningham, Jeff Lacy, Ivan Calderon, Miguel Cotto, and Tim Austin.

When asked about the greatest fight he had worked, Weeks responded without any hesitation or reservation, "The first Diego Corrales vs. Jose Luis Castillo fight." The bout was the 2005 *The Ring* magazine Fight of the Year and the 2005 ESPN Fight of the Year. Hall of Fame announcer Al Bernstein said in a 2005 interview with *Sports Illustrated*, "The most exciting bout—and the one fought on the highest level of any fight I've done in twenty-five years—has to be Diego Corrales and Jose Luis Castillo. It was beyond anything."

In the fight, which was for the WBC lightweight championship, the two warriors stood toe to toe for nine rounds until Castillo brutally floored Corrales twice in the tenth. Corrales got up, landed a miracle shot, badly hurting Castillo, and followed it up with a rally that caused Weeks to step in and award the fight to Corrales by technical knockout. The fight, and the way Weeks handled it, put him on the "A" list of international referees. "That was a history making fight," he said. "It is one of the top ten greatest fights of all time. It was a privilege and an honor to work that fight."

Men's Fitness magazine also lists the fight as the ninth greatest fight of all-time. *Time* lists Corrales vs. Castillo as the sixth greatest fight of all time. *Sports Illustrated* lists the fight as the number ten boxing fight of all time.

One can debate whether refereeing skills are something one is born with or something that one learns, but Tony Weeks has had a rapid, near unparalleled ascent. While he certainly has proven to be a natural, few have demonstrated the level of hard work, dedication, and commitment that Weeks has. This student of the game has quickly established himself as one of boxing's top third men.

33

Sam Williams

Multifaceted Sam Williams brings a wealth of life experiences in and out of the ring into a boxing match. Williams is a retired Detroit police officer and a Marine Corps veteran who served his country in Vietnam. He has extensive sports officiating experience and has been refereeing since the 1980s in the once boxing-rich city of Detroit.

A childhood friend got Williams into boxing. "John Brown and I went to high school together. We refereed JV [junior varsity] basketball, and he wanted to be a boxing referee. He suggested we do it together. I said 'I don't know about boxing,'" recalled Williams, who was in his thirties at the time and had been working out with Brown. But Williams got in the ring anyway to practice refereeing a sparring match with some heavyweights in the gym. His competitive spirit and quest to excel quickly took over. Showing intense dedication and commitment to excellence, Williams honed his new craft. "I got in there, for thirty-five rounds, five days a week, for months," Williams recalled. "The old trainers [in the gym], would always watch and give advice. They told me to keep moving, lest you block a judge, or a fan's view. 'You got paying customers, this is a boxing match,' they would tell me."

After several months, Brown ended up with a promoter's license. He requested Williams referee the fights. Williams did not yet have a referee's license, so he had to go get one. He asked Brown and some others, "How do you know if I am ready?" Brown told him "You've been ready!" He started with Brown's promotion, quickly rose through the ranks, and has not looked back.

Williams had been no stranger to officiating. In addition to refereeing over disputes on the street as a police officer in Detroit (which he did for thirty years before his retirement in 1994), Williams had also refereed football and basketball games. He was an NCAA Division I football referee in the Mid-American Conference for sixteen years, until retiring in 2008.

Williams immediately began refereeing in the professional boxing ranks before the amateur, a step not often taken. His first title fight was August 15, 1986, with Detroit's Jimmy Paul retaining his IBF lightweight title in his third defense against former conqueror Darryl Tyson over fifteen rounds. The fight was held at Cobo Arena in Detroit. Williams has worked many memorable bouts over the years and has traveled outside the United States to act as the third man in the ring in Italy, Germany, Colombia, South Korea, South Africa, the United Kingdom, and Ecuador. When asked which fights stand out, he said, "You never forget your first title fight. Jimmy Paul and Darryl Tyson is a fight I will always remember.

"I remember my second title fight as well. It was in Korea, and two Korean fighters boxed," continued Williams of the December 1986 fight between Jum-Hwan Choi and Cho-Woon Park for the IBF 108 pound title. "I remember one of the fighters kept hitting the other guy low, and then he kept bowing to me every time I warned him. It just kept happening over and over. Of course, I don't speak Korean, so I just scolded him and told him, 'You better stop bowing, he's going get in your butt!'

"Another fight I remember was Oba Carr and Livingstone Bramble," said Williams of the *USA Tuesday Night Fights* 1991 classic between young lion and cagey veteran. The nineteen-year-old Carr was 20-0 and considered the best prospect in boxing—headlining the event against former champ Livingstone Bramble in the monstrous Auburn Hills Palace. Bramble was thought to be done but surprised many by flooring Carr twice, with Carr squeaking out a close ten-round decision. Carr is considered by many to be one of the best modern-era fighters never to win a world title.

"It was like man versus boy," Williams recalled. "Bramble had so much strength. Every time they clinched, you could see the expression on Carr's face. Carr had the speed; he was more polished and quicker. That was what got him through."

The fight between Wladimir Klitschko and Lamon Brewster was "the most gentlemanly and easiest fight I ever refereed," Williams said of the July 7, 2007, rematch in Germany. Brewster had dramatically stopped Klitschko in 2004 to win the WBO heavyweight title. The rematch, televised on HBO, featured an improved Klitschko and an aged Brewster. "Those guys were gentlemen. Just clean fighters. Originally, the Brewster camp had problems with me," recalled Williams. "They didn't know me by face, just that I was from Detroit. Klitschko's trainer, Emmanuel Steward, he is from Detroit, from the Kronk gym. I remember I walked in, and Brewster saw me, and he smiled and said, 'Man, we are not going to have any problems.' He recognized me; I had refereed his fights in the amateurs. He had fought in Michigan before, he was [former heavyweight champ and Olympian, from Flint, Michigan] Chris Byrd's cousin. He knew I would do a good job refereeing him, and be fair."

Williams also refereed a December 1994 title fight between Bernard Hopkins and Segundo Mercado in Quito, Ecuador. Hopkins had previously unsuccessfully challenged Roy Jones Jr. for the middleweight title, and was fighting on unfriendly turf in Mercado's home country. Hopkins went down to the hard punching Mercado twice, in the fifth and the seventh round—it was the first time Hopkins had ever been knocked down in his professional career. The bout was scored a draw, but many believe that Hopkins should have won, despite the knockdowns.

"I didn't know much about Hopkins. I had seen a little of Mercado. I got in to Ecuador the day before, and Bernard must have beat me by about three-four hours," recalled Williams. "He showed himself to be a real warrior. By the end of the second or third round, I remember Hopkins breathing real heavily. And I thought, *oh man, we're going to have a quick knockout.* The air was so thin there, it was pitiful! But after that, it was if someone had wound him up. Every time [Mercado] came in, Hopkins would give it to him. After the fight was over, Hopkins held his head down, when it was announced it was a draw. I told him, 'hey, hold your head up.' Now, when I see him, we always laugh, and remember we go way back together."

Four months later, Hopkins would win by a knockout in a rematch over Mercado in the United States to win the IBF middleweight title. Even Williams, however, could not imagine that, almost seventeen years after that match, Hopkins would become the oldest boxing champion in history, beating Jean Pascal for the WBC light heavyweight title.

Lloyd Honeyghan and Johnny Bumphus is another fight that stands out in Williams' mind. The two fought for the IBF and WBC welterweight titles in February 1987, and the bout was shown on national TV in the United States and Great Britain. The undefeated Honeyghan was one of the hottest fighters in boxing, having just knocked out Donald Curry, one of the top pound-for-pound fighters. He was expected to have a challenge in former junior welterweight titlist Bumphus. "Everyone thought that was going to be a competitive fight. But you could really see fire in Honeyghan's eyes," said Williams. "I will never forget that look.

"There were a lot of things going on behind the scenes as well. The BBBC [British Board of Boxing Control] wouldn't let the IBF sanction the fight. This was one of the last real big title fights on free TV. It was out in Wembley with a ton of people there. Once we started, there were differences that no one told us about. In the United States, they signal with ten seconds before the break in rounds is left. In Britain, they do it with five seconds.

"In the first round, Bumphus went down hard from a punch. He was all right, but he looked like he didn't want to continue. I told him it was a championship fight, to get up. I guess I talked him into it," recalled Williams. "I've learned a lot since then. Between the first and the second rounds, when they signaled with five seconds left, some guy was tugging on my pants as I was in the corner waiting for the round to start [it was the cameraman, telling him to get out of the way]. When I turned to tell him not to tug on my pants, the bell rang, and Honeyghan jumped across the ring before the corner man of Bumphus could get out of the ring, and knocked him down again. I stopped the fight, and gave Bumphus time to recover. Everyone started booing, which being from law enforcement, I was used to.

"Under championship rules, I could have disqualified [Honeyghan], but I took a point off," said Williams. "I let it continue, but I had to stop it a short time later. Bumphus just didn't have the heart for that fight. I learned, if someone doesn't have the heart, you have to stop the fight."

Williams has certain rules that he would advise all referees to follow. "Watch the boxers. No one else concerns you. Inside the ring, the boxers are what you pay attention to. You are in there to referee two boxers competing against each other. They deserve your undivided attention." Other cardinal rules for Williams are to, "always keep yourself in position by the fighter's open side. You can't always be there. But you can be in position to see what's going on. Know your boxers, know their tendencies, if possible. If you watch them work for a while, things will show. You don't want to get behind the fighter—they will foul. Some fighters look to get you out of position, so they can foul."

Williams also commented on a common boxing trick, and referee mistake: "A lot of fighters do not like [getting hit with] body shots, so they grab the punches of their opponents low. They knock a totally legal punch down and make it look illegal. Sometimes a referee will stop and give a fighter a warning, and he didn't see the punch. We have all seen it on television. So you want to be in position to see these things," said Williams about the importance of being in the right position to see what is a low blow, and what is a legitimate body punch.

"Be fit. Stay in shape. Being objective [is important]. Be slow to jump to conclusions. Things aren't always what they appear to be," suggested Williams. "Make sure you see what you are supposed to see. You have a young man's, or woman's life, in there, and you have to pay attention. You want to make sure no one is hurt badly."

Williams feels that his experience as a police officer and his experiences in the military greatly aid him in his role as a boxing referee. "You are always decision making, both in the police and in the military. A referee has to be a decision maker. I've made life or death decisions. I have no problems making them."

ABOUT THE AUTHORS

Mike Fitzgerald has authored five previous boxing books including former heavyweight champion Ken Norton's book *Going the Distance* (2000), and boxing's knockout leader Archie Moore's biography, *The Ageless Warrior* (2004). Fitzgerald has been a licensed professional boxing judge since 1992 and has officiated title bouts in several states and abroad, including Australia, South Africa, and North Korea. He lives in Janesville, Wisconsin, with his wife, Deb, and his two children—son Ross and daughter Allie.

Patrick Morley is an attorney in Chicago, Illinois, where he resides with his wife, Chantall. He is a former Chicago police officer and sergeant. He is an adjunct faculty member at several universities, teaching legal and investigative classes, and has written two textbooks on criminal justice. He is also a licensed professional boxing and mixed martial arts judge who has officiated world title fights in both sports.